To my mother and father,
all my family and friends,
Kim, Louis, Jill, Lyndon, Annie,
Isobel, Martin, Yvonne and Johnny
With love

THE VEGETABLE MARKET COOKBOOK

CLASSIC RECIPES FROM AROUND THE WORLD

COLLECTED & ILLUSTRATED BY ROBERT BUDWIG

TEN SPEED PRESS

10

Ten Speed Press
P.O. Box 7123
Berkeley, California 94707

Text and cover design by Robert Budwig
Illustrations copyright © 1993 by Robert Budwig
Copyedited by Lee Faber
Production by Edward Allhusen, Old House Books
Typesetting by Townsend Typesetter Ltd

First published in Great Britain by Rosendale Press Ltd,
Premier House, 10 Greycoat Place, London SWlP lSB

Library of Congress Cataloging in Publication Data
Budwig, Robert.
The vegetable market cookbook / written and
illustrated by Robert Budwig
        p.   cm.
        Includes index
        ISBN 0-898 15-498-7
1. Cookery, International. 2. Cookery (Vegetables) I.
        Title. TX725.A1B82 1992
        641.6'5 - dc20
        92 - 26114
        CIP

Printed in Italy by G. Canale, SpA

1 2 3 4 5 - 96 95 94 93 92

CONTENTS

INTRODUCTION

*A*s a child I always remember going to the local market with my mother and our maid in my hometown of Cali, Colombia. There, a splendid array of exotic tropical vegetables and fruit, fish from the nearby port of Buenaventura, and spices all adorned a large market square filled with the noise and bustle one would expect of a people born with the sun very much part of their everyday life.

My grandparents, who had a hotel and restaurant in the nearby city of Medellin, were an enormous influence on my brothers and myself. They grew many of their own vegetables and herbs and on weekend visits, our grandmother would treat us to delicious local and European food. We would watch her in the kitchen preparing our favourite dishes. My mother, who learned a great deal from her own mother has herself always been a splendid cook, providing a sumptuous dinner in no time at all just as some foreign visitor had made an appearance at our home.

We enjoyed our food so much, even at an early age, that when my parents entertained, my brothers and I devised a basket on a pulley that would bring marvellous goodies from the kitchen up to one of our bedrooms. This avoided the embarrassment of being seen by guests, making our way to the kitchen through the open plan home. The maid would load our basket carefully with delicious left-overs, and we would enjoy our very own feast upstairs. I suspect my mother made that bit extra, knowing we would be disappointed to miss out on any dish.

When we moved from South America to Europe, I discovered the magic of Italian and French markets. The vast selection of Mediterranean produce fascinated me as did the warmth of the market people, who are always passionate about their region, its food and wine. I was instantly attracted to the medieval village squares, filled with colourful umbrellas and boisterous market traders. Here I could be seduced by mounds of sun-ripened tomatoes, rich mauve aubergines, tender fine beans, elegant long artichokes, with not a car in sight! A friendly stall-keeper would offer me a taste of a new cheese or some hitherto unseen fruit, chatting about plans for the evening meal and local ways to use the fresh produce. I would sit myself down with paper and paints and try to capture some of their spirit until lunchtime, when I would just buy myself some good ripe tomatoes and a fresh loaf of bread and enjoy a hearty snack overlooking the market scene.

So my passion for markets grew, and wherever I travelled, it was the markets I searched out. When I visited the country around Marrakesh, in Morocco, I saw many locals coming by donkey from far off hilltop villages to the weekly market. Here, they sold their home-grown produce and purchased essential food supplies that they cannot grow themselves, before their long journey home. Here, I could really see and experience the feeling that food comes from the earth, as I passed fields of cardoons, leeks and onions, that also appear in the nearby market, freshly dug out, and randomly displayed in baskets. Immediately, curiosity is aroused to learn how the people who grow these vegetables transform them in their traditional cooking.

When I saw aubergines growing profusely in Provence, as well as artichokes sprouting from the rich terracotta soil, I felt a real respect for the farmers who with much hard labour, provide us with a marvellous variety of produce. Good, fresh, ripe and seasonal vegetables are at the very heart of the cooking traditions of many countries. The infinite variety provides us with delicious, healthy and usually economical dishes.

The more unusual vegetables that I have included are at the very least worth looking for and in many cases worth making special trips to track down. Certain vegetables, such as sweet potatoes or cardoons, may not look impressive but have a wonderful flavour.

From all my happy hours in markets around the world, I have brought back my drawings of market scenes, of unusual and exotic vegetables and classic recipes from all of these ingenious traditions. Many of these I gathered from market people, friends, professional and amateur cooks. Some of these vegetable dishes are quick and easy to do, others are more elaborate.

I hope that you will have as much fun cooking these dishes at home as I did, and agree with me that there is little that is as enjoyable as preparing food that is to be savoured and shared with friends and family at your table. Happy cooking and Buen Apetito!

Robert Budwig
London

ITALIAN

Markets

*M*arkets are the lifeblood of Italian society. Ever since I first visited Italy, I have been drawn to the markets that take place daily in the larger towns and cities, or weekly in the smaller villages, when local farmers set up simple trestle tables and large sun umbrellas in the main square. I remember waking one morning in San Giminiano, a beautiful walled village in the heart of the Tuscan hills and seeing with surprise every available space in the main square taken up by keen stallholders whereas the previous day there was only a quiet piazza.

Among the hustle and bustle of shoppers were huge bunches of basil with its unique pungent aroma, mauve artichokes displayed in old wicker baskets, aubergines (eggplant), some as large as coconuts, in shades of marvellous deep-purple. The overall impression was one of colour and freshness. Women sought out the reddest tomatoes and the freshest courgette (*zucchini*) flowers and stumbled on huge Amalfi lemons with their aromatic leaves, large purple heads of garlic and rosemary, sage and oregano tied neatly in bunches.

In Rome, I was lucky enough to find a studio in the very heart of Trastevere, one of the oldest parts of the city, a few minutes' walk from San Cosimato market. I awoke at 5 am some mornings to find the local market people setting up their stalls; most of them

SAN COSIMATO MARKET ROME

farmers from the nearby Frascati hills. Immensely friendly, they were quite happy to let me borrow a whole box of broccoli to sketch. I could not resist buying rosemary and sage plants to enhance the view from my studio window, as well as improving a pasta or risotto dish!

One of the market people invited me to his farmhouse out in Frascati to see the harvest of olives being hand-picked by plump, boisterous country women, who laughed and giggled as the day's picking progressed. The women had been picking olives since the very early hours of the morning and would continue to do so throughout the harvest. Although olive oil is now pressed using the latest technology and modern aluminium vats, it was a joy to see the care and attention taken at every stage. Just before lunchtime, I was offered some freshly-grilled bread with a good helping of first cold-pressed olive oil poured over it; a great delight.

In Sicily, the market in Palermo draws anyone interested in food. A long winding path leads down to the market with stalls and shops crammed in on either side, selling everything from nuts, dates and figs from nearby North Africa to vegetables such as *finoccio di montagna*, wild mountain fennel used in the popular *pasta con le sarde*, a pasta dish containing sardines, wild fennel, raisins and pine nuts. Here you will see stalls piled high with all kinds of leaf vegetables, including *rughetta*, which we call rocket or arugula, monk's beard, *barba di cappucino*, and tiny young spinach leaves. I also saw an abundance of large, plump aubergines and so many beefsteak and deep red ripe plum tomatoes I wondered how all the different stalls managed to compete with each other. As I walked further down to the main square, I was surrounded by marvellous displays of fish and shops making *involtini*; a speciality of swordfish, chicken or meat stuffed with herbs and spices on skewers with bay leaves and onions. I couldn't resist buying some to take back to the studio to grill and they were superb!

At a stall piled precariously high with jars of sun-dried tomatoes, preserved peppers and cheeses, the stallkeeper almost hidden by his display, I was offered several samples. As I explored the market, I was next seduced by the aromas from a nearby bakery and soon found myself being shown how the various breads were prepared and baked in the old wood-fired oven. Needless to say, I left with another bag full of samples and enjoyed a lovely lunch sitting near a dilapidated baroque fountain where several Sicilians working nearby were enjoying a break.

As I travelled back to Rome, it seemed as if the entire plane was filled with the aromas of basil, oregano, spiced olives and wild fennel which I had brought with me. I was eager to return to my studio so I could cook some of the Sicilian specialities for my friends and reminisce about the market.

TOMATO & MOZZARELLA SALAD

*A*fter spending a morning sketching in Rome, I would buy a bunch of basil; its fragrant aroma luring me to the stall, and some bright-red, ripe beefsteak tomatoes to prepare this simple classic salad known as *Caprese*, since it originated on the Isle of Capri. It filled me with energy for the afternoon's work. It is an excellent starter and, if using the freshest ingredients, such as a very fine virgin olive oil, moist buffalo mozzarella and fresh basil, it can be a unforgettable experience. Serve with wholemeal crusty Italian bread or a round olive bread.

SERVES 4
4 ripe beefsteak tomatoes
125 g/4$^{1}/_{2}$ oz buffalo mozzarella cheese
12 fresh basil leaves, thinly sliced
60 ml/4 tbsp best-quality virgin olive oil
15 ml/1 tbsp white wine vinegar
5 ml/1 tsp dried oregano
salt and freshly-ground black pepper

Slice the tomatoes thickly and arrange on a serving dish or on individual plates. Slice the mozzarella cheese 5 mm/$^{1}/_{4}$ inch thick and arrange on top of the tomatoes. Mix two-thirds of the basil, olive oil, vinegar, oregano, salt and pepper to taste in a tightly-lidded screw-top jar and pour over the salad. Garnish with the remaining basil just before serving.

COURGETTES WITH MINT

*C*ourgettes (*zucchini*) and mint go very well together in this recipe, which takes only a few minutes to prepare. It is very refreshing served cold as a salad.

SERVES 4
8 medium-sized courgettes
150 ml/5 fl oz olive oil
30 ml/2 tbsp red wine vinegar
2 cloves garlic, crushed
45 ml/3 tbsp fresh chopped mint
salt and freshly-ground black pepper

Wash the courgettes and dry well. Cut into quarters lengthways, then in half across. Heat the oil in a wok or frying pan and fry the courgettes until golden and just cooked through.
Transfer the courgettes and the cooking oil to a bowl or platter and sprinkle with the vinegar, garlic and mint. Season with salt and pepper and serve at room temperature or chilled.

STUFFED COURGETTE FLOWERS

Courgette (*zucchini*) flowers are abundant during the summer months in markets throughout Italy, where they are sold in neat bunches. They are often served stuffed, or used in delicate risottos or in pasta dishes. Outside Italy, gardeners who grow their own courgettes can put the flowers to good use with this recipe; one of the first things I choose to eat when I travel to Italy. Stuffed with mozzarella cheese and anchovies and deep-fried until golden, they make heavenly starters.

SERVES 4

55 g / 2 oz (½ cup) plain white flour
2 eggs, separated
60 ml / 4 tbsp milk
1 clove garlic, crushed
140 g / 5 oz buffalo mozzarella cheese,
   chopped into very fine dice
55 g / 2 oz anchovy fillets, finely chopped
5 ml / 1 tsp finely chopped fresh parsley
12 fresh courgette (*zucchini*) flowers
vegetable oil for deep-frying

First make the batter. In a bowl, mix the flour, egg yolks, milk and garlic until smooth. Whisk the egg whites until stiff and fold gently into the flour mixture until well-combined. Make the stuffing by mixing the mozzarella cheese, anchovies and parsley together in another bowl. Clean the courgette flowers carefully with a damp cloth, gently separating the petals to make sure the flowers are clean inside. Place 5 ml / 1 tsp stuffing inside each flower head, twisting the petals to enclose it. Heat the oil in a deep-fryer or wok to 180°C / 350°C / Mark 4, or until a cube of white bread turns golden in 1 minute. Dip each flower in the batter, making sure all sides are coated. Fry the stuffed flowers in batches for about 1 minute, until crisp and golden on all sides. Remove from the oil and drain on absorbent kitchen paper (paper towels). Continue until all the flowers are fried. Serve immediately.

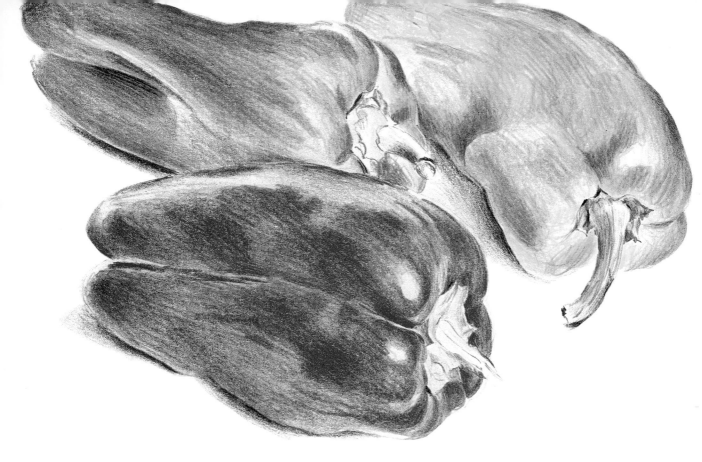

PEPERONATA

A traditional recipe from Sicily, this colourful dish is ideal served with chicken or fish, warm or cold.

SERVES 4
670 g / ¹/₂ lb yellow and red peppers
75 ml / 5 tbsp olive oil
1 medium-sized onion, chopped
2 cloves garlic, crushed
2 stalks celery, chopped
450 g / 1 lb ripe tomatoes, skinned and chopped
3 bay leaves
salt and freshly-ground black pepper

Clean the peppers, remove the seeds and white membrane and cut into small dice.
Heat the oil in a medium-sized heavy saucepan and fry the onion and garlic until the onion begins to turn golden. Add the peppers and celery and fry for 2-3 minutes, then add the tomatoes and bay leaves. Reduce the heat, cover and slowly simmer the vegetables until they are soft, about 35-40 minutes. Discard the bay leaves, season with salt and pepper and serve either hot or cold.

BRUSCHETTA

*B*ruschetta is a simple snack of toasted Italian bread, grilled (broiled) with garlic, olive oil and most often, either tomatoes or black olives. When made with really good olive oil, it can be a treat. While visiting an olive grove in Frascati, the owner offered me memorable *bruschetta*, made with freshly-toasted bread, garlic and newly-pressed olive oil poured over.

SERVES 4

450 g / 1 lb ripe tomatoes, chopped
12 thin slices *ciabatta* or other crusty, bread
2 cloves garlic, peeled
15 ml / 1 tbsp dried oregano
sea salt and freshly-ground black pepper
6 fresh basil leaves, finely chopped to
  garnish

Heat the grill (broiler) and toast the bread lightly on both sides. Rub the bread with the garlic cloves, arrange the tomatoes on the toast, sprinkle with olive oil, oregano, salt and pepper and grill until the tomato is just soft, about 3 minutes. Remove from the grill, sprinkle with chopped basil and serve immediately.

GRILLED AUBERGINES WITH MINT

*D*uring a summer holiday on the island of Ponza, off the west coast of Italy, I often lunched with friends at a restaurant overlooking the sea. Among the selection of *antipasti* offered, this became my favourite; simple, yet totally satisfying. This dish is best prepared one day in advance.

SERVES 6

2 large aubergines (eggplant)
45 ml/3 tbsp olive oil
30 ml/2 tbsp white wine vinegar
2 cloves garlic, crushed
salt and freshly-ground black pepper
24 fresh mint leaves to serve

Wash the aubergines and remove the stems. Slice thinly across, sprinkle generously with salt, put in a colander or sieve and leave for 30 minutes to drain. Meanwhile, prepare the marinade. Mix the oil, vinegar, garlic and a little salt and pepper to taste together in a small bowl. Rinse the aubergines well and pat dry with a tea towel or absorbent kitchen paper (paper towels).
Heat the grill (broiler) and cover a baking tray (cookie sheet) with foil. Place the aubergines on the tray in one layer and grill for 4 minutes. Turn over and grill for a further 3 minutes, until the aubergines are browned. Remove from the grill and arrange on a serving dish. Pour the marinade over, leave to cool, cover with cling film (plastic wrap) and chill in the refrigerator overnight. To serve, sprinkle with mint leaves.

ROCKET & PARMESAN SALAD

*T*he sharp, peppery taste of rocket (arugula) is very good in salads. Fresh parmesan cheese is most important to the success of this recipe, as well as a good-quality olive oil.

SERVES 4

85 g/3 oz (1½ cups) rocket leaves
60 g/2 oz (½ cup) parmesan cheese, thinly shaved
45 g/3 tbsp best quality virgin olive oil
15 ml/1 tbsp white wine vinegar
salt and freshly-ground black pepper

Wash the rocket leaves and drain well. Put into a salad bowl and scatter the parmesan cheese over.
Make the dressing by mixing the oil and vinegar together in a tightly-lidded screw-top jar. Season with salt and pepper to taste. Just before serving, pour over the salad and toss well.

FRIED COURGETTE & AUBERGINE SLICES

*A*nother favourite with friends, these thin slices of courgettes (*zucchini*) and aubergines (eggplant) are terrific served either hot or cold as part of a light lunch.

SERVES 4

450 g / 1 lb courgettes (*zucchini*)
450 g / 1 lb aubergines (eggplant)
plain white flour for coating
2 eggs, well beaten
30 ml / 2 tbsp parmesan cheese
100 g / 3½ oz (1 cup) white breadcrumbs
2.5 ml / ½ tsp dried oregano
pinch of cayenne pepper
150 ml / 5 fl oz olive oil
salt and freshly-ground black pepper
lemon wedges to serve

Wash the courgettes and aubergines. Slice diagonally across, sprinkle the aubergine generously with salt, put in a colander or sieve and leave for 30 minutes to drain. Rinse well and pat dry with absorbent kitchen paper (paper towels).
Put the flour in a bowl. In another bowl, combine the eggs and cheese. In a third bowl, mix the breadcrumbs, oregano and cayenne pepper. Lightly coat the vegetables with flour, then dip into the egg and cheese mixture and finally into the breadcrumbs, making sure the vegetables are well-covered and placing them on a platter until you are ready to deep-fry.
Heat the oil in a frying pan over a moderately-hot heat. Fry the vegetable slices, a few at a time, until they are golden-brown. Remove from the pan with a slotted spoon and drain. Keep warm in the oven until all the vegetables are fried. Serve with lemon wedges.

ROASTED PEPPERS MARINATED IN GARLIC & OIL

*T*hese peppers are ideal as an appetizer served on thin slices of hot *ciabatta* bread. I usually serve a plateful for friends to help themselves. The peppers can be made in advance and kept covered in the refrigerator for a day or two.

SERVES 6-8

800 g / 1¾ lb red and yellow peppers
60 ml / 4 tbsp good-quality olive oil
2 cloves garlic, crushed
30 ml / 2 tbsp white wine vinegar
15 ml / 1 tbsp dried oregano
salt and freshly-ground black pepper
45 ml / 3 tbsp finely chopped fresh parsley

Preheat the oven to 200°C / 400°F / Mark 6. Cut the peppers in half lengthways and remove the seeds and white membranes. Place side by side on a baking tray (cookie sheet) covered with aluminium foil, skin down and bake for about 25 minutes. Turn the peppers over and bake for a further 20 minutes.

Meanwhile, prepare the marinade by mixing the oil, garlic, vinegar, oregano, salt and pepper together in a bowl.

Remove the peppers from the oven, put them in a bowl and leave covered with a tea towel for 20-30 minutes. Remove and peel. Cut each pepper in half lengthways and put in a bowl, pour the marinade over and marinate in the refrigerator, covered preferably overnight.

Before serving, sprinkle with chopped parsley.

MUSHROOM SOUP

*T*he area around Asti, south of Turin, is filled with ancient villages, romantic castles and undulating hills with many vineyards. It was here that I visited "La Contea" restaurant, a haven of Piemontese food, run by Claudia and Tonino Verro, in a lovely old house, with frescoes in the dining room and splendid views of the countryside. Claudia researches traditional Italian recipes and this delicious soup uses dried *funghi porcini* (wild boletus mushrooms) for which this region is well-known. I love the warmth and woody flavour of this soup, which makes a substantial lunch when served with good bread.

SERVES 4

20 g/³⁄₄ oz (¹⁄₄ cup) dried *porcini* (boletus) mushrooms, soaked in a little warm water for 2 hours or overnight
60 ml/4 tbsp extra virgin olive oil
15 ml/¹⁄₂ oz (1 tbsp) butter
225 g/8 oz fresh mushrooms, thinly sliced
1 medium-sized onion, finely chopped
2 cloves garlic, crushed

2 ripe tomatoes, skinned and chopped
1 litre/1¹⁄₂ pints (1 quart) chicken or vegetable stock
salt and freshly-ground black pepper
1 egg
60 ml/4 tbsp freshly-grated parmesan cheese
30 ml/2 tbsp finely chopped fresh parsley
4 thin slices country bread

Drain the mushrooms, reserving the soaking liquid and chop roughly. Heat the oil and butter in a medium-sized heavy saucepan over a moderate heat. Add the dried and fresh mushrooms, onion and garlic and sweat for several minutes. Add the tomatoes, half the mushroom liquid and the stock. Season with salt and pepper and simmer for 15 minutes. Meanwhile, in a small bowl, beat the egg and mix with the parmesan cheese and half the parsley. Heat the grill (broiler) and toast the bread until crisp and golden on both sides.
Remove the mushroom mixture from the heat and allow to cool a little, then add the egg mixture, carefully stirring until the soup thickens.
To serve, place a slice of toasted bread in each individual soup bowl, pour the soup over and garnish with the remaining parsley.

BAKED AUBERGINE WITH MOZZARELLA

*D*uring my visit to the village of Casole d'Elsa, near Siena, I stayed at the Verocchio Summer Arts School, run by Janet and Nigel Konstam. Here we enjoyed simple Italian food, cooked by Mauro Antonello, a local chef, served each evening on the terrace, with panoramic views of the Tuscan hills with their abundant vineyards, elegant cypress trees and historic villages below. Janet was kind enough to share this recipe with me. It makes a hearty main course served with a light salad.

SERVES 4-6

4 medium-sized aubergines (eggplant)
120 ml / 4 fl oz olive oil
1 recipe Italian Tomato Sauce (page 26)
225 g / 8 oz mozzarella cheese, thinly sliced
60 ml / 4 tbsp fresh chopped basil
salt and freshly-ground black pepper
55 g / 2 oz ($\frac{1}{2}$ cup) freshly-grated parmesan
  cheese

Wash the aubergines and remove the stems. Slice thinly lengthways, sprinkle generously with salt, put in a colander or sieve and leave for 30 minutes to drain. Rinse well and pat dry with absorbent kitchen paper (paper towels).

Heat 60 ml / 4 tbsp of the oil in a frying pan over a moderate heat and fry the aubergines, a few slices at a time, until they are golden-brown on both sides. Remove with a slotted spoon and drain on absorbent kitchen paper. Continue frying, adding a little more oil if necessary. Aubergines initially soak up all the oil and as they start softening, they will release it.

Prepare and purée the tomato sauce and heat gently.

Preheat the oven to 200°C / 400°F / Mark 6. To assemble, grease an ovenproof dish and pour a thin layer of tomato sauce in the base.

Arrange a layer of aubergine on the sauce and top with a layer of mozzarella cheese. Sprinkle with chopped basil and season with salt and pepper. Continue layering sauce, aubergine, mozzarella, basil and seasoning until all the ingredients have been used, finishing with a layer of cheese. Sprinkle with freshly-grated parmesan cheese and bake in the oven until the cheese is bubbling and golden-brown, about 20 minutes. Serve piping hot.

STUFFED PEPPERS & AUBERGINES

I first sampled this dish in Rome, cooked for me by Josefina, an Italian housewife I met at the San Cosimato market in Trastevere, the heart of ancient Rome. When she discovered my love for Italian food, she invited me to her home and prepared several of her favourite dishes, including this one, which can either be served as a starter or as a main course with various salads.

SERVES 4

150 ml / 5 fl oz milk

140 g / 5 oz (3 cups) fresh white breadcrumbs

2 large aubergines (eggplant)

2 green or red peppers

90 ml / 3 fl oz olive oil

5 cloves garlic, crushed

450 g / 1 lb ripe tomatoes, skinned, seeded and finely chopped

2 eggs, lightly beaten

12 fresh basil leaves, chopped

18 black olives, stoned (pitted) and finely chopped

75 g / 2½ oz anchovy fillets, finely chopped

30 ml / 2 tbsp chopped capers

30 ml / 2 tbsp finely chopped parsley

15 ml / 1 tbsp dried oregano

55 g / 2 oz (½ cup) freshly grated parmesan cheese

Put the milk in a bowl, add the breadcrumbs and mix. Cut the aubergines in half lengthways and carefully scoop out as much of the flesh as you can with a sharp knife, being careful not to pierce the skins. Sprinkle the shells with salt. Chop the aubergine flesh into small cubes. Cut the peppers in half lengthways and remove the seeds and white membranes.

Heat 30 ml / 2 tbsp of the olive oil in a large frying pan over a moderate heat and fry the garlic, aubergine and tomatoes for 5 minutes, stirring occasionally. Remove from the heat, allow to cool a little and add the beaten eggs, stirring until the mixture is well-incorporated. Add the basil, olives, anchovies, capers, parsley, oregano and parmesan cheese. Mix well.

Preheat the oven to 190°C / 375°F / Mark 5. Drain the breadcrumbs well and stir into the main mixture. Fill the aubergine and pepper shells. Grease an ovenproof dish with 30 ml / 2 tbsp of the olive oil and arrange the stuffed vegetables in one layer. Pour the remaining oil over and bake for 30-35 minutes, or until crisp on top. Serve hot or cold.

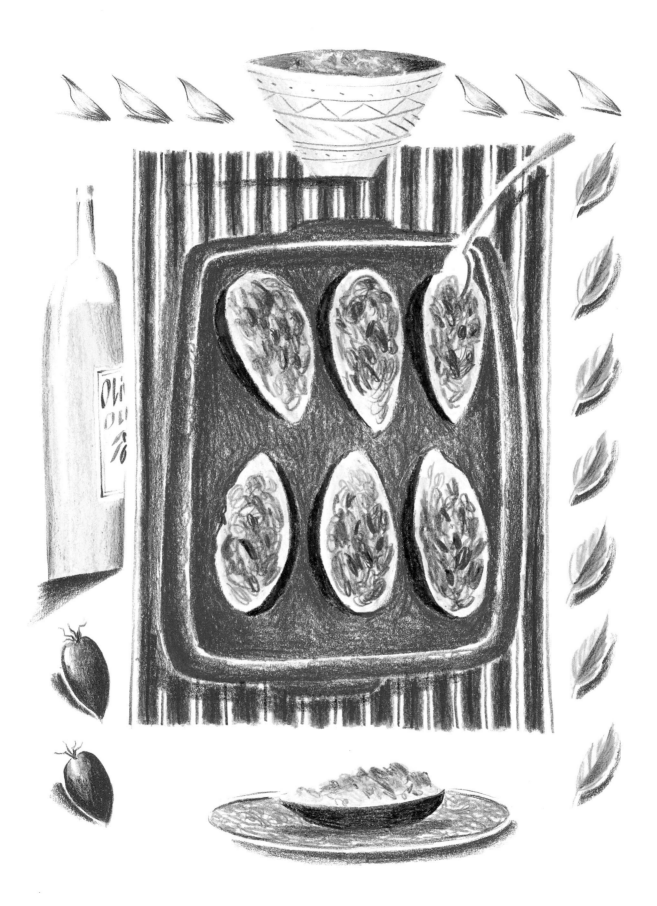

ITALIAN TOMATO SAUCE

*T*his sauce is perfect with pasta, for pizza topping, or as a basis for many other dishes. Use fresh plum tomatoes in the summer when they are abundant, but in winter, use tinned plum tomatoes as they usually have a better flavour than fresh winter tomatoes.

MAKES SUFFICIENT SAUCE FOR 500 g / 1¹/₄ lb PASTA

45 ml olive oil
2 large cloves garlic, crushed
1 medium-sized onion, finely chopped
1 large carrot, peeled and finely chopped
1 stalk celery, finely chopped
450 g / 1 lb fresh plum tomatoes, skinned and chopped *or* 400 g / 14 oz tinned plum tomatoes, chopped

15 ml / 1 tbsp tomato paste
2 bay leaves
salt and freshly-ground black pepper
5 ml / 1 tsp granulated sugar
5 ml / 1 tsp dried oregano
6 fresh basil leaves, chopped

Heat the oil in a medium-sized heavy saucepan over moderate heat and fry the garlic, onion, carrot and celery until the onion is transparent. Add the tomatoes, tomato paste, bay leaves, salt and pepper to taste, sugar and oregano and mix well. Simmer, covered for about 15 minutes, then uncover and cook for a further 15 minutes until vegetables are tender. Discard the bay leaves and add the basil. The sauce should now be fairly thick and ready to serve. If you prefer a smoother sauce, purée in a blender or food processor. Correct the seasoning if necessary.

CAULIFLOWER & ORECCHIETTE

*O*recchiette are small, ear-shaped pasta, most often found in Puglia, the southeast heel of Italy. When I travelled through this marvellously fertile region filled with olive groves, the richest red terracotta soil and hundreds of vineyards, I saw women in the smaller towns of Otranto and Monopoli making fresh orecchiette outside in the narrow streets. Cauliflower is grown profusely here and this recipe is a simple, quick and healthy combination. Broccoli can be used as a variation. Served in the cream-ragged ceramic bowls typical of this region, this pasta looks a treat!

SERVES 6

900 g / 2 lb cauliflower
4 large cloves garlic, peeled
150 ml / 5 fl oz good-quality olive oil
500 g / 1 lb orecchiette or pasta shells
10 anchovies, packed in oil, drained and
  chopped
1 medium-sized onion, finely chopped
5 ml / 1 tsp dried chilli flakes
20 sprigs fresh flat leaf parsley
salt and freshly-ground black pepper

Cut the cauliflower into florets, discarding the stems and put the florets into a large pan of lightly salted boiling water along with 2 of the garlic cloves. Cook for 3 minutes, or until tender. Drain, reserving the cooking water. Discard the garlic and put the cauliflower florets aside. Bring the water back to the boil, add the pasta and cook, following the packet instructions.

Meanwhile, heat the oil in a large saucepan over a moderate heat and add the anchovies. Cook for 1 minute and, with a wooden spoon, mash them into the oil. Add the onions, the remaining garlic, crushed and chilli flakes and fry gently until the onion is transparent.

When the pasta is cooked, drain and transfer to the saucepan containing the anchovy mixture. Add the reserved cauliflower and parsley, mix thoroughly and cook for a further minute until heated through. Serve immediately.

TRENETTE WITH PESTO, BEANS & POTATOES

When I visited Liguria, I enjoyed some delicious food at "A Capeo", a superb restaurant run by Nelly and Franco Solari, with marvellous views of the Ligurian coastline. There I tasted this *trenette al pesto*, the authentic recipe for fine ribbon noodles with basil sauce, served with green beans and potatoes. *Pesto* must be served raw and unheated. It is traditionally made in a pestle and mortar, but it can also be prepared using either a blender or food processor. Pesto will keep indefinitely in the refrigerator if it is stored in an airtight jar, covered over with olive oil.

SERVES 4
2 potatoes, peeled and diced
75 g/3 oz (³/₄ cup) fine green beans, topped
    and tailed and cut into 2.5 cm/
    1 inch pieces
350 g/14 oz trenette
For the pesto:
36 basil leaves, washed and dried
3 cloves garlic, peeled and chopped
55 g/2 oz (¹/₂ cup) pine kernels
pinch of salt
60 ml/4 tbsp freshly-grated parmesan cheese
60 ml/4 tbsp freshly-grated *pecorino* cheese
75 ml/5 tbsp extra virgin olive oil

Place the basil, garlic, pine kernels and a pinch of salt into a food processor or blender and process briefly. (Or pound in a marble mortar using a wooden pestle.) Add the two cheeses and begin to add the oil, a little bit at a time, until the mixture is smooth and creamy. Meanwhile, bring a large saucepan of salted water to the boil. Put in the potatoes and the beans and cook for 5 minutes. Add the pasta to the vegetables and cook, following the packet instructions carefully. When the pasta is cooked *"al dente"* (to the bite), drain and toss with the prepared *pesto* sauce.

RISOTTO WITH SPINACH, PEAS AND MUSHROOMS

A lovely green risotto, superb as a main course served with salad. Risotto must be served immediately after it is cooked, so prepare all the vegetables in advance. Assembly and cooking will take approximately 30 minutes.

SERVES 4

10 g/2 tbsp dried *porcini* (boletus) mushrooms
150 ml/5 fl oz warm water
1 carrot, peeled and cut into small dice
1 stalk celery, cut into small dice
55 g/2 oz (1¼ cups) fresh shelled peas
225 g/8 oz fresh spinach leaves
55 g/2 oz (4 tbsp) butter
1 small onion, finely chopped

225 g/8 oz (1¼ cups) risotto rice, preferably Arborio
120 ml/4 fl oz dry white wine
780 ml/26 fl oz vegetable stock
100 ml/3½ fl oz double (heavy) cream
salt and freshly-ground black pepper
40 g/1½ oz (½ cup) freshly-grated parmesan cheese

First prepare the vegetables. Soak the dried mushrooms in the measured warm water for 1-2 hours.

Meanwhile, cook the carrots, celery and peas separately in a small amount of lightly salted boiling water until just tender. Refresh and drain. Wash the spinach and cook in just the water clinging to the leaves. Drain and chop.

Thirty minutes before serving, drain the dried mushrooms, reserving the soaking liquid.

Melt the butter in a medium-sized heavy saucepan over moderate heat, add the onion and rice, and cook until the onion is transparent. Add the wine and cook until it evaporates. Mix the vegetable stock with the mushroom soaking liquid and add about half to the rice, a little at a time, waiting until it has been absorbed before adding more,. This will take about 10 minutes.

Add the carrots, celery, peas, spinach, dried mushrooms and cream to the rice and season with salt and pepper. Continue cooking, adding stock as needed until the rice is *al dente* (with a "bite"). Add the parmesan cheese at the last minute, stirring vigorously for a minute or two and serve immediately.

Piselli
1480

Porini

2000

SALTORES STALL IN PALERMO·SICILY

HUNTER'S CHICKEN WITH TOMATOES & MUSHROOMS

*T*uscany enjoys a tradition of rich and rugged food. This recipe from Casole d'Elsa in the Chianti region, has a strong and pungent aroma and rich, red colour. This wonderful main course, served with potatoes or bread transports me instantly to the terracotta villages and towns of Tuscany.

SERVES 4-6

20 g/³/₄ oz (¹/₄ cup) dried *porcini* mushrooms

45 g/1¹/₂ oz (3 tbsp) butter

45 ml/3 tbsp olive oil

3 rashers streaky bacon, chopped

3 small onions, chopped

2 cloves garlic, crushed

2 dried red chilli peppers, finely chopped

1.4-1.8 k g/3-4 lb fresh chicken, cut into 6 portions

6 fresh ripe plum tomatoes, skinned and chopped *or* 400 g/14 oz tinned plum tomatoes

15 ml/1 tbsp tomato paste

120 ml/4 fl oz *Chianti* or other dry red wine

salt and freshly-ground black pepper

Soak the mushrooms in warm water to cover for 15 minutes.

Heat one-third of the butter and oil in a large frying pan and fry the bacon until crisp. Add the onion and garlic and cook until they begin to turn golden, then add the chilli. Remove from the heat.

In a second frying pan, heat the remaining butter and oil and brown the chicken portions on all sides, about 10 minutes. Transfer the chicken to the first pan and add the tomatoes, tomato paste, salt and pepper to taste and red wine. Cook over a moderate heat.

Meanwhile, line a sieve with absorbent kitchen paper (paper towels) and strain the mushroom soaking liquid into a bowl. Rinse the mushrooms in fresh water, chop and add to the chicken. Top up the liquid in the pan with the strained mushroom liquid as needed. Cook the chicken for 30 minutes, or until tender. Serve with plain boiled potatoes.

SPINACH GNOCCHI

*T*hese dumplings are so light, they simply melt in the mouth. Serve as a starter, about 5-6 *gnocchi* per person, with butter and plenty of parmesan cheese, or as a light lunch with Italian Tomato Sauce (page 26), accompanied by a hearty salad.

SERVES 6

450 g / 1 lb fresh spinach leaves
salt and freshly-ground black pepper
1.25 ml / ¼ tsp freshly-grated nutmeg
225 g / 8 oz *ricotta* cheese
40 g / 1½ oz (3 tbsp) butter
1 egg plus 1 egg yolk, well-beaten
85 g / 3 oz (¾ cup) plain white flour
30 g / 1 oz (2 tbsp) butter to serve
60 ml / 4 tbsp freshly-grated parmesan cheese

Wash the spinach thoroughly, discarding the stalks and any coarse leaves. Put into a saucepan and cook, with just the water clinging to the leaves, until very tender, about 10-15 minutes.

Sieve the *ricotta* cheese into a bowl. When the spinach is cooked, drain well and squeeze dry. Put into a food processor or blender with the cheese, butter, eggs and flour and process.

Turn the spinach mixture into a bowl. Bring a large pan of salted water to the boil. Preheat the oven to 130°C / 250°F / Mark ½. Prepare a well-floured board and using floured hands, form small dumplings by breaking off small pieces of the spinach mixture onto the floured board and turning to coat all sides with flour. Pick up gently and form a ball between the palms of your hands.(The mixture must be very light and you must take care in handling it.) As you form each ball, lay out on a well-floured dish. When they are done, drop them, a few at a time, into the boiling water for 5 minutes. As they rise to the top of the water and float, remove with a slotted spoon, drain well and slide onto a warmed serving dish. Keep hot in the oven. When all the *gnocchi* are cooked, pour melted butter over. Serve on individual plates with a sprinkling of parmesan cheese.

BAKED FENNEL

*F*ennel is a very versatile vegetable. The following dish may be served either as an excellent starter or as an accompaniment.

SERVES 4

900 g / 2 lb fennel bulbs
55 g / 2 oz (4 tbsp) butter
2.5 ml / ½ tsp freshly-grated nutmeg
salt and freshly-ground black pepper
55 g / 2 oz (½ cup) freshly-grated parmesan
  cheese

Preheat the oven to 200°C / 400°F / Mark 6.
Clean the fennel, discard any bruised leaves and cut off the feathery fronds to use as a garnish. Cut the bulbs in half crossways and cook in lightly salted boiling water until tender, about 10-15 minutes. Drain well.
Butter a shallow ovenproof dish. Add the fennel and sprinkle with nutmeg, salt and pepper. Dot with the remaining butter and sprinkle with the parmesan cheese. Bake in the centre of the oven until just golden, about 10 minutes.
Heat the grill (broiler) to hot. When the fennel is baked, slide under the grill for 2-3 minutes, until browned.
Serve hot, garnished with fennel fronds.

PASTA WITH FUNGHI PORCINI SAUCE

*E*ver since I first saw basketsful of these delectable wild mushrooms in the restaurants of northern Italy, I have not been able to resist stopping at any stall where they are sold to treat myself to a few.
Fresh *funghi porcini* however are hard to find, so dried *porcini* (boletus) mushrooms are a very acceptable substitute.

SERVES 4-6

20 g / ³/₄ oz (¹/₄ cup) dried *porcini* (boletus) mushrooms, soaked in warm water for 1 hour

30 ml / 2 tbsp olive oil

60 ml / 4 tbsp finely chopped fresh parsley

7.5 ml / 1¹/₂ tsp finely chopped fresh rosemary

3 cloves garlic, crushed

120 ml / 4 fl oz dry white wine

300 ml / 10 fl oz double (heavy) cream

salt and freshly-ground black pepper

500g fusilli or fresh tortelloni

fresh basil to garnish

To prepare the sauce, drain the dried mushrooms, retaining the soaking liquid. Heat the oil in a wide, shallow pan over a moderate heat and gently cook the parsley, rosemary and garlic for about 5 minutes. Add the mushrooms, wine and 120 ml / 4 fl oz mushroom soaking liquid. Continue to cook until the liquid has reduced by half. Add the cream and salt and pepper to taste.
Cook the pasta, following the packet directions carefully, in a pan of salted boiling water, drain and mix with the sauce. Serve immediately garnished with basil leaves.

BROCCOLI & COURGETTE LASAGNE

I love green vegetables served together and often prepare a whole dinner party using green as a theme. The fresh pasta in this recipe makes the lasagne light, although dried pasta is a perfectly good alternative.

SERVES 6

For the pasta:
100 g/3½ oz (scant cup) plain flour
3 eggs, lightly beaten
pinch of salt
5 ml/1 tsp olive oil
or 12 sheets fresh or dried green
  lasagne

For the filling:
360 g/13 oz (2¾ cups) courgettes
  (*zucchini*), thinly sliced
450 g/1 lb broccoli, cut into small
  florets

150 ml/5 fl oz *pesto* (page 18)
45 ml/3 tbsp pine kernels
45 ml/3 tbsp chopped walnuts
salt and freshly-ground black pepper
100 g/3½ oz (1 cup) freshly-grated
  parmesan cheese
1 recipe quantity bechamel sauce
  (page 38)

First make the pasta. In a bowl, mix the flour, eggs, salt and olive oil into a rough ball. Then turn out onto a clean, lightly-floured surface and knead until the dough is smooth and elastic, about 10 minutes. Cover with cling film (plastic wrap) and allow to rest about 30 minutes.

Meanwhile, steam the courgettes and broccoli separately for approximately 5-7 minutes, until just tender. Refresh in cold water and drain. Mix with the *pesto* sauce, pine kernels and walnuts and season with salt and pepper.

Cut the pasta dough into four pieces. Roll each piece out individually until it is approximately 30 cm/12 inches square and 2 mm/⅛ inch thick.

Cut into 7.5 cm/3 inch wide strips, then into 12 cm/5 inch lengths.

Cook the lasagne two sheets at a time in a large pan of salted boiling water to which you have added a little olive oil for 2 minutes. Lift out of the pan with a slotted spoon and plunge into a bowl of cold water. Drain and lay out separately on absorbent kitchen paper (paper towels) to dry.

Continue until all the pasta is partly cooked.

Prepare the bechamel sauce. Preheat the oven to 200°C/400°F/Mark 6. Grease a rectangular ovenproof dish with butter and place strips of pasta into the base, slightly overlapping and arrange a layer of vegetables on top. Sprinkle with a little of the parmesan cheese and pour some bechamel sauce over. Continue layering pasta, vegetables, bechamel and parmesan, finishing with a layer of pasta, covered with bechamel and a good sprinkling of parmesan cheese. Dot with a little butter and bake for about 25 minutes, until golden.

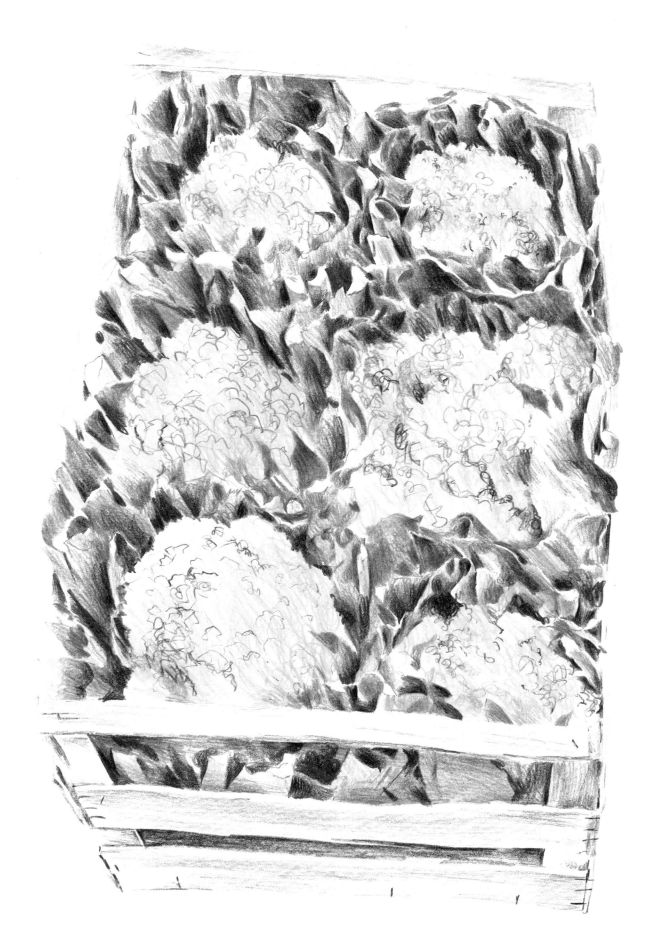

CANNELLONI WITH ASPARAGUS & ARTICHOKES

*W*hen I was in Rome, I noticed an abundance of fresh baby asparagus and artichokes. Antonia, one of the locals at the San Cosimato market, gave me this recipe, which had won her first prize in a local cooking competition. It makes a delicious main course, served with a salad.

SERVES 6

2 globe artichokes
55 g / 2 oz (½ stick) butter
30 ml / 2 tbsp olive oil
1 medium-sized onion, finely
  chopped
3 cloves garlic, crushed
1 dried red chilli (chilli pepper),
  seeded and chopped
120 ml / 4 fl oz dry white wine
salt and freshly-ground black pepper
200 g / 7 oz (about 20 spears) baby
  asparagus
210 ml / 7 fl oz vegetable stock
juice of ½ lemon

55 g / 2 oz (½ cup) freshly-grated
  parmesan cheese
225 g / 8 oz *ricotta* cheese
18 dried cannelloni tubes
For the bechamel sauce:
900 ml / 1½ pints (30 fl oz) milk
1 bay leaf
1 whole clove
sprig of fresh thyme
½ small onion
1.25 ml / ¼ tsp freshly-grated nutmeg
85 g / 3 oz (¾ stick) butter
75 g / 3 oz white flour
salt, freshly-ground black pepper

Prepare the artichokes by removing all the tough outer leaves and cut off the spiky tops. Cut in half, lengthways, remove the choke and discard. Cut the artichoke into thin vertical slices and put into cold water with a squeeze of lemon juice added to prevent discolouration.
Meanwhile, heat the butter and oil in a medium-sized heavy saucepan over a low heat and gently fry the onion, garlic and chilli for 5 minutes. Add the artichokes, stir well and leave to cook for a 10 minutes. Pour in the wine and cook for a further 10 minutes. Season with salt and pepper, add the asparagus, vegetable stock and lemon juice. Cover and simmer for 15 minutes.
Meanwhile, make the bechamel sauce. In a medium-sized, heavy saucepan, put the milk, bay leaf, clove, thyme, onion and nutmeg and bring slowly to the boil. Remove from the heat, cover with a lid and leave to infuse for 15 minutes. Melt the butter in another saucepan over a low heat, stir in the flour and cook for 2 minutes. Strain the milk through a fine sieve into the butter-flour mixture and gradually heat, stirring continuously. Bring to the boil, then simmer for 2-3 minutes and season with salt and pepper. Remove from the heat and keep warm.
Heat the oven to 200°C / 400°F / Mark 6. Add half the parmesan and the ricotta cheese to the artichoke mixture and mix well. Fill the cannelloni tubes by hand or with the aid of a piping bag. Place the filled cannelloni side by side in one layer in a buttered ovenproof dish. Pour the bechamel sauce over and top with the remaining parmesan cheese. Bake for 20 minutes, until golden-brown on top. Serve immediately.

ROSEMARY POTATOES

*D*uring a visit to the Sabatini restaurant in Rome, I watched the chef prepare these potatoes with plenty of rosemary and garlic and the aroma wafted throughout the restaurant. These potatoes are a good accompaniment to lamb or chicken dishes, and excellent when cooked with some of the fat from roasted meat or chicken.

SERVES 4

450 g / 1 lb medium-sized potatoes, peeled
   and cut into 1.2 cm / ¹/₂ inch dice
120 ml / 4 fl oz olive oil or fat from roasted
   meat or chicken
8 large cloves garlic, peeled
4-5 sprigs fresh rosemary
salt and freshly-ground black pepper

Preheat the oven to 200°C / 400°F / Mark 6. Blanch the potatoes in salted boiling water for 2 minutes. Drain. Heat the oil or fat in a roasting tin with the garlic in the oven for about 5 minutes. Strip the rosemary from the stalks and chop finely. When the oil is hot, put in the potatoes, half the rosemary and season with salt and pepper. Toss the potatoes in the hot oil to coat. Cook for 40 minutes, or until golden, turning once or twice so that the potatoes cook evenly.

When the potatoes are cooked to a golden colour, remove from the oven, place in a serving dish and sprinkle with the remaining rosemary.

ASPARAGUS & PANCETTA

*A*sparagus is such a delicate vegetable that simmering it until just tender and serving with a little melted butter is often sufficient. In Italy, I found baby asparagus served with parmesan cheese and *pancetta* (an Italian unsmoked bacon), which adds an unusual flavour. Try it as a starter, serving about 6 spears per person.

SERVES 4

450 g / 1 lb baby asparagus
30 g / 1 oz (2 tbsp) butter
55 g / 2 oz (2 slices) *pancetta or* streaky unsmoked bacon
90 ml / 3 oz (1 cup) freshly-grated parmesan cheese
salt and freshly-ground black pepper

Cut off any tough parts of the asparagus stems. In a pan of lightly salted boiling water, cook the asparagus quickly until tender. Refresh under cold running water and drain. Arrange in a buttered baking dish in one layer.
In a small frying pan, melt the butter and gently fry the *pancetta* until crisp. Remove from the heat.
Preheat the oven to 200°C / 400°F / Mark 6. Dot the asparagus with butter and sprinkle with parmesan cheese. Bake in the oven for 5 minutes, until the cheese melts.
Serve with the *pancetta* crumbled over the asparagus.

CAPONATA

*T*his Sicilian recipe featuring aubergines (eggplant) and olives, makes an appetizing starter, especially when accompanied with *ciabatta* bread, grilled (broiled) with a little olive oil and sprinkled with oregano. *Caponata* can be made in advance and reheated or served cold.

SERVES 6

1 kg / 2 lb aubergines (eggplant), diced
75 ml / 5 tbsp olive oil for frying
1 large onion, chopped
1 kg / 2 lb ripe tomatoes, skinned, seeded and chopped
115 ml / 4 fl oz white wine vinegar
45 ml / 3 tbsp sugar
salt and freshly-ground black pepper

1 head celery, thinly sliced
2 small courgettes, diced
60 g / 2 oz (1¼ cups) green olives, stoned (pitted) and chopped
30 g / 1 oz (¼ cup) capers, rinsed and dried
4 anchovy fillets, chopped
30 ml / 2 tbsp pine kernels
15 ml / 1 tbsp chopped fresh parsley to garnish

Sprinkle the aubergines generously with salt, put in a colander or sieve and leave for 30 minutes to drain. Rinse and dry thoroughly.
In a medium-sized saucepan, heat 30 ml / 2 tbsp olive oil and fry the

onions gently until golden. Add the tomatoes and cook until pulpy, then add the vinegar, sugar and salt and pepper to taste. Reduce the heat and simmer, uncovered, to reduce and thicken.

Meanwhile, in a frying pan, heat the remaining oil and fry the aubergines, celery and courgettes for 1 minute. Add to the tomato sauce and leave to stew gently for about 30 minutes, stirring occasionally to prevent the vegetables from sticking to the pan. Add the olives, capers, anchovies and pine kernels and simmer for a further 15 minutes. Check and correct the seasoning.

Serve warm or cold, garnished with parsley.

PIZZA WITH TOMATO & ONION

*M*y preferred pizzas are those that have thin and crispy bases and simple toppings of the freshest vegetables. Here is one of my best-liked from Naples, home of the pizza, where almost every restaurant is a *pizzeria* and the wood-fired ovens work day and night.

MAKES 4 25 CM/10INCH PIZZAS
For the dough:
15 g/½ oz dried yeast
75 ml/3 fl oz warm water
5 ml/1 tsp sugar
450 g/1 lb (4 cups) strong white flour, sifted
30 ml/2 tbsp olive oil
5 ml/1 tsp salt
4-5 tbsp warm water
For the topping:
1 recipe quantity Italian Tomato Sauce
  (page 26)
2 medium-sized onions, finely sliced
24 anchovy fillets
10 ml/2 tsp dried oregano
60 ml/4 tbsp olive oil
12 pitted black olives

First prepare the dough. Sprinkle the dried yeast and sugar into a bowl with 3 fl oz of warm water. Whisk thoroughly and leave to rise in a draught-free place until frothy, about 15 minutes.
Place the flour in a large bowl and make a well in the centre. Pour in the yeast, oil and salt and mix well. Make a rough ball, adding warm water until the bowl is clean. Turn onto a lightly floured surface and knead until smooth and elastic, about 5 minutes. Form into a ball, put back into the bowl, pour another small spoonful of oil over the top, cover with a damp tea towel and leave to rise in a warm place for 1-2 hours, until doubled in volume.
Meanwhile, prepare the tomato sauce. Once the dough has risen, knead briefly again and divide into 4 pieces and roll into balls.
Preheat the oven to 230°C/450°F/Gas 8. Roll the pizza bases out one at a time on a lightly floured surface into a circle approximately 25 cm/10 inches in diameter.Place each base on an oiled pizza pan or nonstick oven tray and spread two spoonsful of tomato sauce over each one.
Arrange the onion slices on top and place 4 anchovy fillets and olives on each pizza in a cross pattern. Sprinkle with oregano and a little olive oil.
Bake for 10-15 minutes until the edges become golden-brown.
Serve immediately.

BEETROOT PASTA

*I*n this, the simplest and most unusual of pasta dishes, the beetroot gives an incredible pink colour to the sauce. This recipe, first prepared for me by Lina, who runs an *enoteca* or wine bar in Trastevere, Rome, can be prepared in almost no time at all.

SERVES 4

225 g/8 oz cooked beetroot (beets)
2 cloves garlic, crushed
15 ml/1 tbsp fresh lemon juice
300 ml/10 fl oz thick double (heavy) cream
5 ml/1 tsp balsamic vinegar
5 ml/1 tsp Dijon mustard
sea salt and freshly-ground black pepper
400 g/14 oz *farfalle* (bow-ties)
15 ml/1 tbsp olive oil (optional)
4 slices streaky bacon, thinly sliced
(optional)

Put the beetroot, garlic, lemon juice and half the cream into a food processor or blender and process until smooth. Put the mixture into a medium-sized saucepan over a low heat, add the remaining cream and heat through for about 8-10 minutes, but do not allow to boil. Add the vinegar, mustard, salt and plenty of pepper. Stir well and keep over a low heat.

Put the *farfalle* into a large pan of salted boiling water and cook, following the packet instructions. Meanwhile, if you are using the bacon, heat the oil in a separate pan and fry the bacon until crisp and golden. Drain on absorbent kitchen paper (paper towels).

When the pasta is cooked, drain well and stir into the sauce. Mix well and serve with the bacon sprinkled on top.

PUMPKIN RISOTTO

*T*his risotto, with its wonderful orange colour and subtle taste, is ideal during the autumn months when pumpkin is so abundant in the markets.

SERVES 4

15 ml / ¹/₂ oz (1 tbsp) butter
15 ml / 1 tbsp olive oil
1 large onion, finely chopped
1 carrot, peeled and chopped
1 stalk celery, chopped
4 rashers streaky bacon, chopped
450 g / 1 lb pumpkin, peeled and cut
  into very small cubes

280 g / 10 oz (1¹/₂ cups) risotto rice,
  preferably Arborio
600 ml / 1 pint (2¹/₂ cups) chicken or
  vegetable stock
120 ml / 4 fl oz dry white wine
100 g / 3 ¹/₂ oz (1 cup) freshly-grated
  parmesan cheese

Heat the butter and oil in a medium-sized heavy saucepan over a low heat. Add the onion, carrot, celery and bacon and fry for 10 minutes until lightly browned. Remove from the heat and purée in a blender or food processor. Return the mixture to the rinsed out pan.
Add the pumpkin and cook gently for five minutes then add the rice. In a separate saucepan, heat the stock to simmering point and add the wine.
Add the wine-stock mixture to the main saucepan in 150 ml / 5 fl oz quantities, waiting until the liquid has been absorbed before adding more. When you have approximately 150 ml / 5 fl oz liquid left, the rice should be *al dente* (with a "bite"), but if you prefer a creamier-textured risotto, add the remaining wine and stock.
Just before serving, add the parmesan cheese, stirring vigorously for a minute or two.

FRENCH
Markets

*D*uring one of my first visits to France, I drove with friends through Brittany and Normandy exploring medieval villages and staying with friendly farmers who provided us with simple accommodation and delicious regional home cooking. On our first expedition to the nearest town, we found ourselves in a traffic jam and soon realized that it was market day! I was amazed at the sight of the town square and the roads leading up to it filled with umbrellas of canvas in a multitude of colours; sociable shoppers ready with their wicker baskets, eager to find the freshest fennel or best bunch of garlic, all carefully inspected by both husband and wife. We could not resist being caught up in all this activity and bought a wonderful array of local produce for a picnic lunch. It was hard to decide which of the twenty or so varieties of chèvre cheese we should buy until a helpful Frenchwoman advised us of her favourite, which, we discovered later, was absolutely delicious. Nor could we resist a few olives marinated in *herbes de Provence* or others marinated in garlic and dill.

I eagerly inspected huge bunches of leeks, with all their green foliage, just dug out from the soil that morning, which I thought would be perfect for a quick still life drawing, after which I could prepare a simple *poireaux vinaigrette* (page 62), an absolute favourite of mine. I noticed a great variety of onions; white, red, torpedo-shaped brown and the tiniest shallots and inspected squashes and gourds; some of which were edible and others, shaped like swans, which were just wonderful to look at. Bunches of garlic were neatly strung up for the most part and piled high in white, smoky and mauve colours with huge cloves. There were boxes of streaky pink beans and artichokes, neatly packed or loose with their long stalks and prickly leaves. There were also stalls selling home-made honey: acacia, lavender, sunflower, chestnut and several other varieties with hand-written labels.

On a recent journey through Provence and its markets, I travelled through the most amazing countryside, hillsides covered with olive trees, tiny villages with pink, sun-weathered roof tiles and pastel walls, when I noticed vast fields of flowering artichoke plants. I stopped immediately to inspect this marvellous sight and saw numerous artichoke blossoms rising from long stems in a particularly elegant and striking way. I was so keen to sketch some of these specimens, I could not resist cutting a few, leaving speedily afterward for fear of being caught by some enraged farmer! After sitting on my terrace drawing artichokes, I made them into a soup and sat watching the sun set beyond the hills and the vast valley below, reflecting on one of my most satisfying days: an unexpected visit to a farm; a lively market where people were happy to share old family recipes and finally, cooking my freshly-picked vegetables.

TAPENADE

*T*his Provençal spread makes a good appetizer served on thin slices of toasted bread, decorated with basil leaves or thin slices of lemon. It can also make an unusual filling for baked potato.

SERVES 6
400 g / 14 oz pitted black olives
2 cloves garlic, crushed
4 anchovy fillets
15 ml / 1 tbsp capers, drained
juice of ½ lemon
30 ml / 2 tbsp extra virgin olive oil
pinch of sea salt
freshly-ground black pepper
toasted bread to serve
basil leaves or lemon slices to garnish

Put the olives, garlic, anchovies and capers in a blender or food processor with half the lemon juice and blend at high speed for 30 seconds, then start adding the olive oil in a thin stream and continue blending until you have a smooth paste. (You may have to scrape the mixture down, using a rubber spatula.) Add salt and a generous grinding of black pepper and the remaining lemon juice to taste.
Spoon into a serving bowl, cover with cling film and refrigerate for 1-2 hours before serving.

RADISHES WITH BREAD

*D*uring a brief stay in Hornfleur, I visited a 14th century market square filled with ancient wooden stalls, manned by old and young traders with rugged country faces and friendly, beaming smiles. I stopped there to admire traysful of long red and white radishes, which traditionally are served very simply in France, just dipped into salt and eaten with French bread and good quality butter (unsalted). But, of course, the radishes must be very young and crisp I was advised.

SERVES 4-6
1 bunch fresh radishes
55 g / 2 oz (¹/₂ stick) unsalted butter
1 French loaf
coarse sea salt

Wash the radishes. Trim, leaving a small "handle" of leaves. Serve with top-quality unsalted butter, freshly baked French bread and coarse sea salt. Each ingredient must be in perfect condition to achieve the point of this simple hors d'oeuvre.
Alternatively, the radishes may be thinly sliced and arranged on little rounds of buttered French bread, sprinkled with salt.

LEEK & POTATO SOUP

A perfect combination, this soup can be served hot or chilled. When cold, it is known as Vichyssoise.

SERVES 4-6
900 g / 2 lb leeks
55 g / 2 oz ½ stick) butter
450 g / 1 lb potatoes, peeled and diced
1 stalk celery, chopped
600 ml / 1 pint (2½ cups) chicken or
    vegetable stock
600 ml / 1 pint (2½ cups) milk
salt and freshly-ground black pepper
freshly-grated nutmeg
300 ml / 10 fl oz double (heavy) cream
45 ml / 3 tbsp finely-cut fresh chives

Wash the leeks 2-3 times and drain. Thinly slice the white part, plus 5 cm / 2 inches of the green.
Melt the butter in a large saucepan over a moderate heat and add the leeks and potatoes. Cook for 7 minutes, stirring continuously. Add the celery, pour over the stock and milk and bring to the boil. Reduce the heat to a simmer and season with salt, pepper and nutmeg. Simmer for 25 minutes, until the vegetables are tender.
If serving hot, stir in the cream and correct the seasoning. Heat through, but do not allow to boil. Remove from the heat. (I prefer tasting the texture of the vegetables, but you can puree it if you like). To serve cold, process in a blender or food processor, add the cream and correct the seasoning. Allow to cool, then chill in the refrigerator until cold. Garnish with chives.

ROAST ONION & AUBERGINE

*T*his recipe is quick and easy to prepare, but needs good-quality olive oil.

SERVES 4
1 large onion, peeled and cut into wedges
1 large aubergine, cut into thin slices
120 ml / 4 fl oz good-quality olive oil
sea salt and freshly-ground black pepper
few sprigs fresh rosemary

Preheat the oven to 200°C / 400°F / Mark 6.
Arrange the onion and aubergine alternately in an ovenproof dish. Dribble with olive oil and sprinkle with salt and pepper. Scatter the rosemary on top and roast for 20 minutes, or until the vegetables are soft and golden. Serve immediately.

ONION SOUP

*T*his traditional soup always reminds me of small Paris bistros, where boisterous Parisiennes indulge in large bowlsful. One of the simplest soups to prepare, this can be made in advance, then reheated, with the cheese and croutons added at the last moment.

SERVES 6-8

60 ml / 2 oz (¹/₂ stick) butter

30 ml / 2 tbsp vegetable oil

900 g / 2 lb onions, peeled and thinly
    sliced

5 ml / 1 tsp salt

1.8 litres/3 pints (2 quarts) chicken or
    vegetable stock

5 ml / 1 tsp fresh thyme or
    2.5 ml / ¹/₂ tsp dried thyme

20 ml / 1¹/₂ tbsp plain white flour

120 ml / 4 fl oz water

6-8 slices crusty French bread, cut
    1.25 cm / ¹/₂ inch thick

10 ml / 2 tsp olive oil

1 clove garlic, cut in half

225 g / 8 oz (2 cups) grated gruyere
    cheese

Heat the butter and oil in a large, heavy saucepan over a low heat. Add the onions and salt and cook, covered for about 15 minutes, until the onions are soft and transparent. Remove the lid, increase the heat to moderate and continue cooking, stirring occasionally, until the onions are golden-brown. (I allow them to brown quite a lot as it is this stage that gives the soup added taste and colour.) Stir in the stock and thyme, replace the lid and simmer for 30 minutes. Remove from the heat and allow to cool for 30 minutes.

In a small bowl, mix the flour with the measured water until completely amalgamated. Add to the soup, return to the heat and stir until it comes to the boil. Reduce the heat, simmer for 2-3 minutes until the soup has thickened, then remove the pan from the heat.
Meanwhile, prepare the croutons. Preheat the oven to 200°C/400°F/ Mark 6. Spread the bread out in one layer on a baking tray and bake for 15 minutes on one side. With a pastry brush, lightly coat both sides of the bread with olive oil. Turn the slices round and bake the untoasted side for a further 15 minutes, until the bread is completely dry and lightly browned. Rub each slice with the cut garlic and set aside.
To serve, heat the grill (broiler), place the croutons on the bottom of individual soup bowls, pour the soup over and sprinkle generously with the cheese. If desired place the soup bowls quickly under the grill to melt the cheese.

PISTOU SOUP

*T*his nourishing summer soup, bursting with fresh vegetables, needs to be prepared when you can obtain huge bunches of fresh basil, which gives the soup its name. Pistou, like its Italian counterpart, pesto, is a combination of basil, olive oil and garlic.

SERVES 6-8

15 ml/1 tbsp olive oil
2 medium-sized onions, roughly chopped
2.25 litres/4 pints (2½ quarts) water
225 g/8 oz carrots, peeled and diced
115 g/4 oz leeks, trimmed and sliced
225 g/8 oz tomatoes, skinned and coarsely chopped
2 medium-sized potatoes, peeled and diced
115 g/4 oz (½ cup) fresh or dried white haricot beans
4 stalks celery, thinly sliced
sea salt and freshly-ground black pepper

115 g/4 oz (1 cup) small pasta shapes
225 g/8 oz fine French beans (green beans), topped and tailed
225 g/8 of courgettes (zucchini), sliced
For the pistou:
36 basil leaves
5 cloves garlic, peeled
55 g/2 oz (½ cup) freshly-grated gruyère cheese
sea salt and freshly-ground black pepper
90 ml/3 fl oz good-quality olive oil
grated gruyère cheese to serve

Heat the oil in a large cast iron pot over a moderate heat and fry the onion until it just begins to brown. Add the water, carrots, leeks, tomatoes, potatoes, haricot beans, celery, salt and pepper. Bring to the boil, reduce the heat and simmer, covered, for 45 minutes. Add the pasta, French beans, courgettes and saffron. Cook for a further 15 minutes. While the soup is simmering, prepare the pistou. In a pestle and mortar or food processor, blend the basil, garlic and gruyäre cheese, gradually adding the oil. Set aside. When the soup is cooked, remove from the heat, add the pistou and stir well. Leave for 5 minutes, then serve with additional grated gruyère cheese.

ARTICHOKE SOUP

A fresh-tasting soup that makes the work of cleaning artichokes more than worth the effort.

SERVES 6

2 medium-sized artichokes
1 parsnip, peeled and cubed
1 small onion, chopped
3 stalks celery, thinly sliced
1 small turnip, peeled and cubed
1 small leek, thinly sliced
45 ml/3 tbsp fresh finely-chopped
 parsley
15 ml/1 tbsp lemon juice
1.5 litres/2½ pints (6 cups) chicken
 or vegetable stock

210 ml/7 fl oz water
60 ml/2 fl oz dry white wine
4 ml/¾ tsp dried marjoram
1.25 ml/¼ tsp ground coriander
salt and freshly-ground black pepper
60 ml/2 fl oz single (light) cream to
 garnish
45 ml/3 tbsp shelled pistachio nuts,
 roasted, to garnish

Cut off the artichoke stems and the pointed parts of the leaves, snapping off the tough bottom leaves and discard. Cut the artichokes into quarters. Remove and discard the chokes and inner leaves. Immediately place the cut artichokes into a bowl of water to which you have added lemon juice to prevent discolouration.

Prepare all the remaining vegetables and put into a large, heavy saucepan with the artichokes, stock, measured water, wine, spices and seasoning and bring to the boil over a moderate heat. Reduce the heat and simmer, covered, for 2 hours. Remove from the heat.

Puree the solids with a small amount of the liquid in a food processor or blender in batches. Strain the puree through a medium sieve into the rinsed out pan. Mix well and check and correct the seasoning if necessary.

Roast the pistachios by simply putting them, dry, into a small frying pan and tossing them until golden-brown.

Reheat the soup before serving. Pour into individual bowls and garnish with the cream, dribbled onto the surface in a circular motion with a few pistachio nuts on top.

LEEK TART

A delicate tart with a light, crumbly pastry, this is excellent served warm with salads or cold for a picnic or buffet party. Sometimes I make small tartlets to serve with drinks. Using the same quantities as in this recipe, you can make 24 7.5 cm / 3 inch tartlets.

SERVES 6
For the pastry:
150 g / 5 oz (1¼ cups) fine plain white flour
pinch of salt
7.5 ml / 1½ tsp dried thyme
7.5 ml / 1½ tsp poppy seeds (optional)
115 g / 4 oz (1 stick) butter, diced
30 ml / 2 tbsp iced water
For the filling:
670 g / 1½ lb young leeks
55 g / 2 oz (½ stick) butter
2 egg yolks
30 ml / 2 tbsp double (heavy) cream
30 g / 1 oz (¼ cup) grated gruyere cheese

First make the pastry. Combine the flour, salt, thyme, poppy seeds if using and butter in a food processor or bowl until crumbly. Add the water slowly and work until the dough holds together. Wrap in cling film (plastic wrap) and place in the refrigerator for 30 minutes.
Preheat the oven to 200°C / 400°F / Mark 6. Roll out the pastry on a lightly floured surface to a 30 cm / 12 inch circle and use to line a 25 cm / 10 inch lightly buttered flan tin. Cut out a 30 cm / 12 inch circle of greaseproof paper, place on top of the pastry and fill with dried beans or rice. Bake blind for 10-15 minutes, until the pastry is just baked, but now brown.
Remove from the oven and lift off the weighted greaseproof paper. Meanwhile, prepare the filling. Wash and trim the leeks, slice them thinly and put into a saucepan with the butter over a low heat. Cook gently until the leeks are transparent and very tender, about 10-15 minutes. Add a little water if necessary, but do not allow them to brown. Remove from the heat and cool.
In a bowl, whisk the egg yolks with the cream and add to the leeks. Pour the mixture into the pastry case and smooth the surface. Sprinkle with the gruyere cheese and bake for 15-20 minutes, until the filling is set and lightly browned. The pastry case can be made in advance or the tart can be baked in advance and reheated.

TOMATOES PROVENCAL

A simple, classic Provencal recipe, this is best made using large, ripe tomatoes. When visiting Provence, I spent a morning with hardworking local farmers, picking tomatoes in vast fields and came to realize just how much hand labour is still in use today.

SERVES 4

2 large ripe tomatoes
3 cloves garlic, crushed
55 g/2 oz (1 cup) fresh white breadcrumbs
    (preferably from a French baguette)
15 ml/1 tbsp fresh finely-chopped parsley
1 small onion, finely chopped
7.5 ml/1½ tsp fresh thyme
salt and freshly-ground black pepper
45 ml/3 tbsp olive oil

Preheat the oven to 200°C/400°F/Mark 6. Wash the tomatoes and cut in half horizontally. Mix together the garlic, breadcrumbs, parsley, onion, thyme, salt and pepper. Spread about 15 ml/1 tbsp of the breadcrumb mixture onto each tomato half. Spread about 15 ml/1 tbsp of the oil evenly in a small ovenproof dish and arrange the tomatoes, cut sides up. Dribble with the remainder of the oil. Bake for 15-20 minutes. Serve either hot or cold.

AUBERGINE CAVIAR

*T*his deliciously light hors d'oeuvre can be served in a bowl with a few sprigs of flat parsley and is particularly good eaten with French bread.

SERVES 4

1 large aubergine (eggplant)
salt and freshly-ground black pepper
juice of ½ lemon
3 large cloves garlic, chopped
30 ml/2 tbsp olive oil
1 tomato, skinned, seeded and chopped
pinch of oregano

Preheat the oven to 160°C/325°F/Mark 3. Prick and bake the whole unpeeled aubergine for 1 hour, until tender. Remove from the oven and allow to cool. Scoop the aubergine flesh into a blender or food processor. Add salt and pepper to taste, a little of the lemon juice and the garlic and process until well-mixed. Slowly add the oil. Add the tomato and oregano and blend again. Check for seasoning and add more lemon juice if needed. Serve either in a bowl or on individual plates with French bread.

RATATOUILLE

*T*here are so many variations of ratatouille, but my favourite was cooked by Madame d'Isle during a visit to Bormes les Mimosas on the Cote d'Azur. After a glorious morning by the sea, I would return to lunch of delicious fish awaiting me on the terrace with salads of the freshest ingredients and ratatouille with its distinctive Mediterranean taste. While others would indulge in a siesta, I spent the afternoon sketching. Ratatouille is perfect served warm the day it is prepared. It is equally as good the next day, served cold.

SERVES 4-6

60 ml / 4 tbsp olive oil
450 g / 1 lb ripe tomatoes, chopped
2-3 large onions, sliced
2 large cloves garlic, chopped
450 g / 1 lb aubergines (eggplant), roughly
    sliced
450 g / 1 lb courgettes (zucchini), roughly
    sliced
3 peppers, preferably red, yellow and green,
    seeded and cut into quarters
salt and freshly-ground black pepper

Heat the oil in a large heavy saucepan over a moderate heat. Add the tomatoes first, then add the onions, garlic, aubergines, courgettes, peppers and season with salt and pepper. Cover the pan and cook until the vegetables are reduced to a thick stew. (Apart from the tomatoes and onions, the other vegetables should retain an identifiable shape.) Remove from the heat and correct the seasoning.

Serve as a first course, an accompaniment to meat or fish or as a main dish.

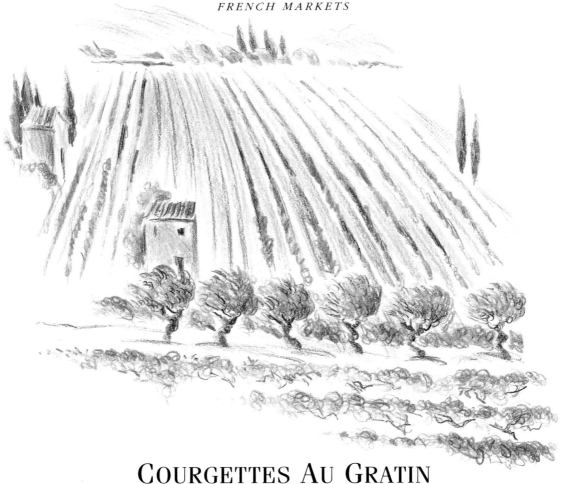

COURGETTES AU GRATIN

A classic way to serve courgettes, this dish is a good accompaniment to grilled or roasted meat. This gratin method can also be adapted to other delicately flavoured vegetables, such as leeks.

SERVES 6
3 kg / 6½ lb courgettes (zucchini)
55 g / 2 oz (½ stick) butter
210 ml / 7 fl oz single (light) cream
200 g / 7 oz (1¾ cups) freshly-grated gruyere
   cheese
salt and freshly-ground black pepper

Peel the courgettes and cut into fine slices. Grease a gratin dish. Melt the remaining butter in a large saucepan over a low heat and add the courgettes. Cook to soften, stirring occasionally, but do not allow to brown. When the courgettes are soft, remove from the heat. Process in a blender or food processor with the cream and half the cheese. Season with salt and pepper and pour into a buttered gratin dish. Preheat the oven to 200°C / 400°F / Mark 6. Sprinkle the remaining cheese over the gratin and cook in the oven for 10 minutes, until the cheese is melted and the gratin is golden-brown.

CELERIAC REMOULADE

*D*uring one glorious week spent concentrating on yoga with friends in the Valley of Roussin, near Angouleme in southwest France, I enjoyed delicious dinners on the terrace after our exercises. My yoga teacher, Dominique and her daughter, Sophie, prepared simple and healthy food for us and the remoulade is particularly special, in my opinion, served with a plate of salami and cheeses, or simply with other salads.

SERVES 4
450 g / 1 lb celeriac (celery root or oyster
  plant)
juice of ½ lemon
For the mayonnaise:
1 egg yolk
60 ml / 4 tbsp white wine vinegar
5 ml / 1 tsp Dijon mustard
salt and freshly-ground black pepper
240 ml / 8 fl oz grapeseed oil

Peel the celeriac and cut into quarters, then into very thin slices. In a medium-sized saucepan, blanch in boiling water with the lemon juice for 2-3 minutes. Remove from the heat, refresh under cold running water and drain. Cut into small match-sticks.

Making mayonnaise is very straightforward and foolproof in a food processor. Place the egg yolk, vinegar, mustard, salt and pepper in the container and blend. Slowly add the oil, a few drops at a time at first, then in a thin stream until all the oil is used. If the mixture becomes too thick, add a few drops of hot water. In a bowl, mix the celeriac thoroughly with the mayonnaise. Chill in the refrigerator and serve cold.

BABY VEGETABLES WITH AIOLI

*T*his is the perfect summer appetizer, when young vegetables are in season. The thick and rich aioli mayonnaise is rather garlicky, so adjust the quantity of garlic to taste.

SERVES 4-6

12 small carrots
10 small courgettes (zucchini)
10 small turnips
225 g/8 of fine green beans
225 g/8 of small leeks, trimmed
1 small cauliflower, cut into florets

For the aioli:

6-8 cloves garlic, peeled and crushed
3 egg yolks
pinch of sea salt
5 ml/1 tsp Dijon mustard
480 ml/16 fl oz of extra virgin olive oil
10 ml/2 tsp lemon juice

Cook all the vegetables separately in a small quantity of lightly-salted boiling water until just tender. Drain and keep warm.
To prepare the aioli, put the garlic, egg yolks, salt and mustard into a blender or food processor and process until smooth. Add the lemon juice, process again and slowly add the olive oil in a thin stream, until you have a smooth mayonnaise and all the olive oil is used. If it seems too thick, add a little extra lemon juice or warm water. Scrape into a bowl and refrigerate until ready to serve.
Arrange the vegetables on a large serving dish and place the aioli in a small bowl in the center, so that everyone can dip the vegetables of their choice into the mayonnaise.

BABY LEEKS VINAIGRETTE

*T*his is a very simple, but delicious first course. If baby leeks are not available, use ordinary leeks, cut into thin slices.

SERVES 4

670 g/1½ lb baby leeks
5 ml/1 tsp hazelnut oil
60 ml/4 tbsp extra virgin olive oil
10 ml/2 tsp sherry vinegar
10 ml/2 tsp red wine vinegar

sea salt and freshly-ground black
  pepper
15 ml/1 tbsp finely-chopped parsley
5 ml/1 tsp coarse-grained mustard

Wash and trim the leeks. Bring a large saucepan of lightly-salted water to the boil and add the leeks. Cook for just under 5 minutes, until tender, but not too soft. Remove from the heat and plunge into cold water to prevent further cooking. Drain and lay on a tea towel to dry.
Make the vinaigrette by mixing all the remaining ingredients together in a glass jar with a tightly-fitting lid.
Arrange the leeks in a serving dish or on individual plates. Pour the vinaigrette over while they are still warm and serve immediately.

RED CABBAGE WITH APPLES

*T*his unusual sweet and sour dish comes from Alsace. It is one of my favourites on a cold winter day.

SERVES 6
1 small red cabbage
60 ml / 2 oz (¹/₂ stick) butter
1 medium-sized onion, chopped
1 large cooking apple, pared, cored and
    sliced
30 ml / 2 tbsp brown sugar
2.5 ml / ¹/₂ tsp ground cloves
juice of 1 lemon
30 ml / 2 tbsp seedless raisins
120 ml / 4 fl oz dry red wine
sea salt and freshly-ground black pepper

Shred or slice the cabbage, then wash and drain.
Melt the butter in a medium-sized heavy saucepan over a moderate heat and cook the onion until transparent. Add the apple, sugar, cloves, lemon juice and raisins and cook for 10 minutes, until the apple is soft. Add the cabbage and wine and cook gently, turning occasionally, until the cabbage is cooked, about 45 minutes.
Serve as an accompaniment to meat or rice.

ASPARAGUS & ROQUEFORT

*T*his dish from northern France makes a very elegant first course with its creamy cheese sauce. Although roquefort cheese has quite a strong taste, it enhances the subtle asparagus flavour.

SERVES 4
500 g / 1 lb fresh young asparagus
150 ml / 5 fl oz double (heavy) cream
30 g / 1 oz (2 tbsp) roquefort cheese,
    crumbled
salt and freshly-ground black pepper

Clean the asparagus, remove any tough, woody stalk-ends and either steam or cook in lightly-salted boiling water until just tender. Drain.
In a small saucepan over a very low heat, cook the cream and cheese until the cheese has melted. Season to taste.
To serve, place a few asparagus spears on each individual plate and pour a little sauce over.

ARTICHOKES PROVENCAL

*T*his is a superb starter, especially if you can find the very small Mediterranean-type purple artichokes. If these are not available, use the hearts only of larger artichokes.

SERVES 4
6 baby artichokes or hearts of 6 large globe
  artichokes
juice of 1 lemon
30 ml/2 tbsp olive oil
1 medium-sized onion, finely chopped
sprig of fresh thyme or 5 ml/1 tsp dried
  thyme
2 bay leaves
sea salt and freshly-ground black pepper
240 ml/8 fl oz dry white wine

Cut the leaf tips off the baby artichokes and trim off the tough outer leaves. Cut each artichoke in half and remove the choke. Alternatively, if using large artichokes, cut out the hearts, reserving the remainder for another use. Immediately drop cut artichokes into a bowl of water to which you have added the lemon juice to prevent discolouration.
Heat the olive oil in a large frying pan over a low heat. Add the onion, drained artichokes, herbs, salt and pepper and wine. Cook, covered for 45 minutes, or until tender, stirring from time to time. Serve warm or at room temperature.

MUSSELS & TOMATOES PROVENCAL

I enjoyed a bowlful of these delectable mussels with friends on the terrace of a small bistro in the village of Lourmarin, Provence. Every time I make them in London, I remember the picturesque village square beside the bistro where the old men play boules.

SERVES 4

1 litre / 2 pints (1 quart) mussels
180 ml / 6 fl oz good-quality olive oil
4-5 ripe plum tomatoes, skinned and
    roughly chopped
4 cloves garlic, finely chopped
30 ml / 2 tbsp finely-chopped fresh parsley
pinch of salt

Soak the mussels in cold water for 30 minutes. Scrub well, discarding any mussels that are open.

Heat the oil gently in a large frying pan and add the tomatoes, garlic, parsley and mussels. Cover and cook over a moderate heat until the mussels open, then cook for a further 5 minutes. Remove the mussels with a slotted spoon and cook the sauce, uncovered, for a further 5 minutes over a low heat.

To serve, remove any unopened mussels and discard. Place the mussels in individual serving bowls and pour the tomato sauce over. Serve immediately.

WARM MUSHROOM SALAD

*T*his salad has an exquisite flavour. Now that so many different varieties of mushrooms can be found in our markets, almost any combination can be used.

SERVES 4

250 g/8 oz mushrooms, such as
   chanterelles, shiitake, chestnut and oyster
   mushrooms
90 ml/3 fl oz walnut or hazelnut oil
1 shallot, peeled and finely diced
1 clove garlic, finely chopped
salt and freshly-ground black pepper
3 young lettuces (choose 1 each from: lollo
   rosso, radicchio, curly endive, butterhead,
   cos, little gem)
sprigs of fresh tarragon, fennel or chervil,
   finely chopped
30 ml/2 tbsp raspberry vinegar

Clean the mushrooms with a damp cloth and cut into manageable pieces. Heat a spoonful of oil in a medium-sized saucepan over a moderate heat, add the shallot and garlic and cook for about 3 minutes, until soft, but not coloured. Add the mushrooms and cook until tender, about 3-5 minutes. Season with salt and pepper.

Wash and dry the lettuces and place with the herbs in a large salad bowl. Pour the mushrooms with the garlic and shallot and pan juices onto the leaves. Heat the remainder of the oil and dribble over the salad. Finally, bubble up the vinegar in the same saucepan, reduce by half, pour over the salad, correct the seasoning and toss well.

Serve warm with French bread.

SALADE NICOISE

On a visit to the town of Apt, which boasts a magnificent market, I found stalls laden with rich black and green olives in a myriad of dressings. I also saw the freshest of goats' cheeses, vibrant red tomatoes and picturesque flower stalls. On the terrace of a nearby restaurant, I sampled a very hearty salade niçoise. It was crunchy, light, yet filling.Serve it with fresh, warm French bread and a glass of chilled white wine to make a very satisfying lunch.

SERVES 4

340 g/12 oz firm tomatoes, quartered
225 g/8 oz fine French beans (green beans), topped and tailed and cut into 2.5 cm/1inch lengths
1 lettuce heart, shredded
200 g/7 oz tin tuna fish
12 anchovy fillets
1 green pepper, pith removed and seeded, thinly sliced
115 g/4 oz small black olives

4 spring onions (scallions), trimmed and thinly sliced
2 hard-boiled eggs, quartered
For the dressing:
90 ml/3 fl oz extra virgin olive oil
2 cloves garlic, crushed
sea salt and freshly-ground black pepper
6 fresh basil leaves, chopped

Sprinkle the tomatoes with salt and set aside to drain.
Wash the beans and cook in a small quantity of lightly-salted boiling water until just tender, about 5 minutes. Plunge into cold water to prevent further cooking, drain and set aside to cool.
Prepare the dressing by mixing all the ingredients together in a glass jar with a tightly-fitting lid. Pour half the dressing into a serving bowl and toss with the lettuce and beans.
Drain the tuna fish, flake and arrange, with the anchovy fillets, olives, green pepper and onion, on top of the lettuce and beans. Arrange the tomatoes and eggs around the edge of the bowl. Sprinkle over the remaining dressing and serve immediately.

CHICKEN WITH 40 CLOVES OF GARLIC

*T*his chicken has a marvellous aroma of garlic and lemon, as you would expect and is very tender. The garlic is not only edible, but a great treat to eat.

SERVES 4
4-5 whole heads garlic
1.75 kg/3½ lb free-range chicken
1 lemon
sea salt and freshly-ground black pepper
1-2 sprigs French tarragon
15 g/½ oz (1 tbsp) butter
15 ml/1 tbsp olive oil
15 ml/1 tbsp brandy
75 ml/2½ fl oz dry white wine

Preheat the oven to 190°C/375°F/Mark 5. Separate the garlic into cloves. It is not necessary to peel them. Remove the excess fat from the chicken cavity and neck and discard. Cut the lemon in half and squeeze the juice from one half. Rub the chicken all over with the lemon juice and place the half lemon inside the cavity of the chicken. Lightly season the chicken inside and out and put one sprig of the tarragon in the cavity. Heat the butter and oil in a large flameproof casserole dish and brown the chicken on all sides over a moderate heat. Pour on the brandy and ignite. When the flames die down, tuck the garlic cloves around and under the chicken and pour over the wine. Cover the casserole and cook in the preheated oven for about 75 minutes.
The chicken can be served as is, with the clear juices and garlic cloves, or a creamy sauce can be made by pushing the unpeeled garlic through a sieve over a bowl, which will leave the skins behind.

R. BUDWIG

POTATOES & BLACK OLIVES

A dish from the Provence countryside, these potatoes take very little time to prepare and are delicious with grilled fish or chicken. Good quality black olives preserved with herbs give the best results.

SERVES 4

30 ml / 2 tbsp olive oil
8 cloves garlic, peeled and roughly chopped
200 g / 7 oz black olives with herbs (see below)
4 bay leaves
1 kg / 2 lb small potatoes, peeled and diced
sea salt and freshly-ground black pepper

Heat the olive oil in a terracotta or cast iron pot over a moderate heat and add the garlic, olives and bay leaves. Stir and cook for 5 minutes. Add the potatoes, salt and pepper and about 2.5 cm / 1 inch water. Cook, covered, for 20 minutes until the potatoes are tender. Remove from the heat and serve immediately.

If you cannot buy prepared herbed olives, it is simple to do yourself, but it must be done at least 24 hours in advance to give the herbs a chance to flavour the olives. Pack the olives in a large glass jar with a tightly-fitting lid. Add a spoonful of good-quality olive oil and 15 ml / 1 tbsp *herbes de Provence*. Marinate the olives for at least 24 hours, giving the jar a shake every hour or so. When the olives are used up, use the oil as the base of a delicious salad dressing.

STUFFED MUSHROOMS

*M*y neighbours Evelyn and Alain spend most summers in central France and each year bring back traditional recipes, including the following mushroom dish, which they serve either as a substantial first course or as a light lunch with an accompanying salad.

SERVES 4

4 large field mushrooms
3 cloves garlic, crushed
1 red onion, finely chopped
2 slices lean bacon, chopped
30 ml / 2 tbsp finely-chopped fresh parsley
25 ml / 1½ tbsp finely-chopped fresh marjoram
25 ml / 1½ tbsp finely-chopped fresh thyme
15 g / ½ oz (¼ cup) fresh white breadcrumbs
sea salt and freshly-ground black pepper
30 g / 1 oz (¼ cup) freshly-grated gruyere cheese
60 ml / 4 tbsp olive oil

Preheat the oven to 200°C/400°F/Mark 6. Wipe the mushrooms clean
with a damp cloth, remove the stems and reserve.
Chop the mushroom stems and put into a bowl with the garlic, onion,
bacon, parsley, marjoram, thyme, breadcrumbs, salt and pepper.
Divide the mixture into quarters and pack into the mushroom caps.
Grease an ovenproof dish with 15 ml/1 tbsp olive oil. Place the stuffed
mushrooms in the dish and sprinkle with the cheese. Dribble the
remaining oil over the mushrooms. Bake for 20-30 minutes and serve hot.

MOROCCAN
Markets

One of my first visits to Morocco was to the old port town of Essouira, which lies directly west of Marrakech. As I travelled to the coast, I passed vast groves of orange and lemon trees, in bloom and bearing fruit, with wonderful aromas drifting my way. Olive groves are scattered all along the way and country folk sell baskets full of freshly picked olives by the roadside. Essouira was designed by a Portuguese who had been captured there. During his long days behind bars, so the story goes, he designed this fascinating walled town which still retains many of the original architectural features, including the cannons that protected the town. At the Villa Maroc, an old 17th century house which has been converted into a marvellous hotel, the cook, Amina, will happily prepare any Moroccan speciality you may care to try and will, if you so desire, take you to the magnificent market nearby, where you can choose fresh produce of all kinds for your feast in the evening.

The *souk* is reached by walking through a terracotta plastered arched gateway to the cobbled main street. Here the vegetables and fruits are displayed on stalls that are painted a light pink or yellow on

MARKET IN ESSOUIRA · MOROCCO

the inside and have wooden turquoise-coloured doorways. The stalls are laden with fresh bunches of small beetroot, mauve-green thistle-like cardoons – a speciality here – piles of carrots, freshly picked and still with all their foliage, turnips, large red and white radishes, pumpkin, quinces, huge pomegranates, sweet potatoes and, of course, there are numerous stalls with piles of very juicy oranges and tangerines, all still with their foliage from the nearby groves. Ladies in colourful *celabas* of bright pinks, rich mauves and light, acid greens are seen talking with their friends, catching up on the local gossip and plans for the evening supper. They carefully choose the nicest bunch of onions or garlic and have a quick chat with the stall-keeper who no doubt they see most days. Most of the women wear a veil over their nose and mouth and look very exotic as you see them glide in their long costumes through the market, baskets filled with their purchases.

As you carry on through the market, there are fresh mint sellers, who set up their tiny stalls on the pavement and sell their strongly-perfumed produce for deliciously refreshing mint tea which is drunk all over Morocco. Individuals hawk baskets of cinnamon sticks. Then come the spice stalls, laden with beautifully arranged pyramids of ground cumin, one of the basic flavours of Moroccan cooking, as well as chilli and turmeric. There are mountains of black and light-pink olives; the latter most often used in *tajines*. Here also you will find the sharp, pickled lemons so popular and important when cooking certain traditional dishes like Chicken with Olives and Lemon (page 83). Other stalls display a wide variety of lentils, dried pulses and chick-peas, along with many varieties of grain, such as cracked wheat and semolina couscous.

I have never been able to resist bringing jars of these specialities back home with me and my hand luggage, consisting of several colourful hand-made wicker baskets, usually ends up looking like a mini-market, with cardoons sticking out of one end and favourite spices, such   as cumin, wafting their aroma to   other passengers nearby!

TOMATO & GREEN PEPPER SALAD

*T*his salad is delicious as a cold starter served with hot, crusty bread or served warm as an accompaniment to fish.

SERVES 4-6

3 green peppers
4 ripe tomatoes
¹/₄ preserved lemon (page 84)
2 cloves garlic, peeled and crushed
pinch of sweet paprika
2.5 ml / ¹/₂ tsp ground cumin
30 ml / ¹/₂ tbsp olive oil
15 ml / 1 tbsp lemon juice
5 ml / 1 tsp salt
7.5 ml / ¹/₂ tsp freshly-ground black pepper

Grill the peppers as on page 21, remove their skins, cut into small cubes and set aside.
Place the tomatoes in a bowl. Boil some water, pour over the tomatoes and leave for 15-20 seconds. Drain the tomatoes and cut off their stems. Slip the skins off, cut in half and remove the seeds. Cut the tomato flesh into small cubes about 1 cm / ³/₈ inch square.
Rinse the preserved lemon under running water and remove the pulp. Cut the rind into small cubes. Arrange the peppers, tomatoes and preserved lemon rind in a dish. Mix together the remaining ingredients to make a dressing and pour over the salad. Mix well.

HARIRA SOUP

*T*his is the traditional soup of Morocco and although it is enjoyed all year round, it is particularly popular during the Ramadan Festival, served after a day's fasting accompanied by dates or honey pastries. It is a deliciously warming soup and very comforting for anyone on a cold winter's day.
In the markets of Morocco, you find stalls just serving Harira soup in beautifully simple decorated bowls, and you see the locals with their hand-carved wooden spoons tucking in.

SERVES 6

60 ml/4 tbsp sunflower oil
1 clove garlic, finely chopped
1 large Spanish onion, finely chopped
30 ml/2 tbsp chopped flat leaf parsley
30 ml/2 tbsp chopped celery leaves
15 ml/1 tbsp salt
5 ml/1 tsp ground black pepper
2 pinches powdered saffron
5 ml/1 tsp ground ginger
30 ml/2 tbsp sweet paprika
30 ml/2 tbsp finely chopped fresh coriander
125 g/4 oz ($\frac{1}{2}$ cup) dried chick peas, soaked overnight or 250 g/8 oz (2$\frac{1}{2}$ cups) tinned chick peas

180 g/6 oz (scant cup) green lentils
60 g/2 oz ($\frac{1}{4}$ cup) yellow split peas
60 g/2 oz ($\frac{1}{4}$ cup) short-grain rice
800 g/28 oz tinned Italian plum tomatoes
1.8 litres/3 pints (2 quarts) chicken or vegetable stock
70 g/2$\frac{1}{2}$ oz (5 tbsp) tomato purée (paste)
60 g/2 oz ($\frac{1}{2}$ cup) plain white flour
120 ml/4 fl oz water
60 ml/tbsp lemon juice
1 lemon, cut into 8 wedges

Heat the oil in a large, deep saucepan or stockpot over a moderate heat. Add the garlic, onion, parsley, celery leaves, salt, pepper, ginger, saffron and paprika. Fry until the onions are transparent. Put the coriander in a pestle and mortar or blender with a little water and pound into a purée.
Add the soaked chick peas (if using tinned chick peas, add only 10 minutes before serving), lentils, split peas, barley or rice to the saucepan and stir well.
Meanwhile, put the tomatoes into a food processor or blender and blend until smooth. Add to the saucepan with the puréed coriander, reduce the heat, cover and cook for 10 minutes.
Warm the stock and add the tomato purée. Stir into the soup and bring to the boil. Cover the pan and simmer for 45 minutes until the chick peas are well-cooked.
Mix the flour with the water to make a runny paste and once all the vegetables are cooked, stir into the soup, stirring continuously to thicken. Continue to cook for a further 10 minutes, adding the lemon juice at the end. Serve with lemon wedges and good crusty bread.

CARROT SALAD

A simple, clean-tasting salad, ideal for summer days and quick and easy to prepare. This also makes a delicious starter if served with the Beetroot Salad and Tomato and Green Pepper Salad (page 77) in separate bowls.

SERVES 4
450 g / 1 lb carrots
1 clove garlic
pinch of ground cinnamon
2.5 ml / ½ tsp ground cumin
pinch of cayenne pepper
juice of 1 lemon
1.25 ml / ¼ tsp granulated sugar
salt and freshly-ground pepper
15 ml / 1 tbsp olive oil
15 ml / 1 tbsp finely chopped
   flat leaf parsley

Peel the carrots and boil whole in water with the garlic for about 7 minutes, or until just tender. Drain, discard the garlic and cut the carrots into .6 cm / ¼ inch thick slices. Mix together the remaining ingredients (except the parsley) to make a dressing and pour over the carrots.
Leave to marinate in the refrigerator for at least 1 hour, covered with cling film (plastic wrap). Garnish with the parsley and serve.

BEETROOT SALAD

I first had this deliciously simple salad in the "Palais Salam" hotel, Taroundant, where, as a starter, you are presented with a marvellous array of small bowls containing different salads and freshly ground cumin to sprinkle on your selection.

SERVES 4-6
900 g / 2 lb raw or cooked
   whole beetroot (beets)
15 ml / 1 tbsp granulated sugar
juice of 1 lemon
15 ml / 1 tbsp olive oil
1.25 ml / ¼ tsp ground cumin
pinch of sweet paprika
15 ml / 1 tbsp finely chopped
   flat leaf parsley

If using raw beetroot, clean and cut off all but 2.5 cm / 1 inch of stalk. Put the beetroot into a pan with enough salted water to cover. Bring to the boil and cook, covered, until tender, about 1 hour, adding more water if necessary. Drain and set aside until cool enough to handle. Slip off the beetroot skins, trim the tops and dice.
Mix together the remaining ingredients to make a dressing, pour over the beetroot and mix well. Leave to chill and serve.

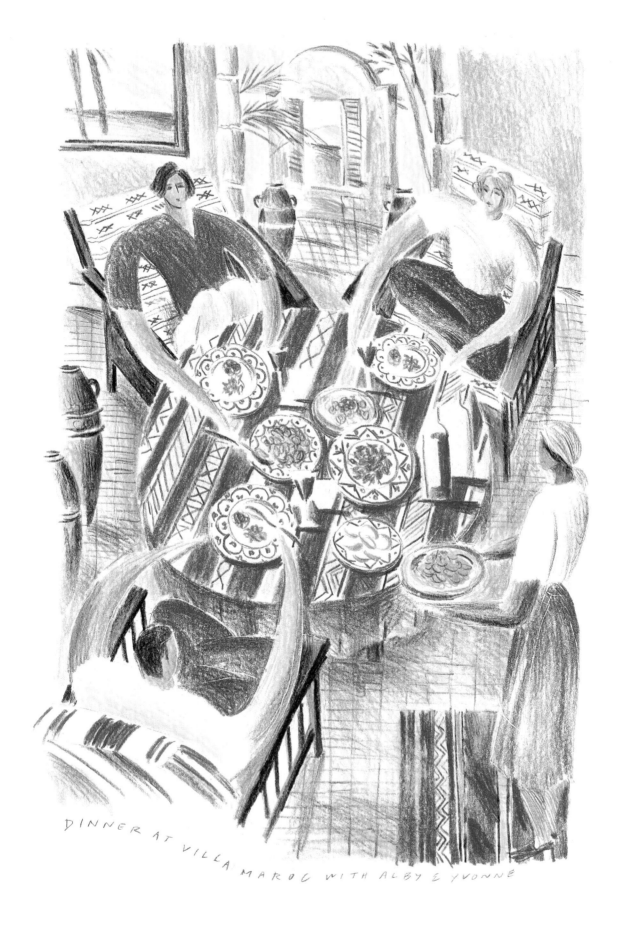

DINNER AT VILLA MAROC WITH ALBY & YVONNE

CHICKEN WITH OLIVES & LEMON

*T*his is one of my favourite ways of preparing chicken with an interesting and delicious combination of flavours. This recipe is usually prepared in a *tajine*, a Moroccan triangular-lidded earthenware dish, but I use a cast-iron lidded casserole.

Preserved lemon adds a very distinctive Moroccan taste to countless dishes and you will find jars of preserved lemons sold all over Morocco in friendly stalls that also sell a huge variety of olives. You can make your own preserved lemons by following the recipe on page 84. You cannot really substitute their flavour with anything else, The first stage of this recipe, marinating the chicken, can be done a day in advance, which makes it perfect for dinner parties, served with plain couscous or boiled rice.

SERVES 4

4 chicken breasts
45 ml / 3 tbsp sunflower oil
2 medium-sized onions, finely chopped
1 beefsteak tomato, skinned, seeded and finely chopped
250 g / 8 oz green or pinkish-brown olives
2 preserved lemons
juice of 1 lemon

For the marinade:
30 ml / 2 tbsp sunflower oil
6 cloves garlic, finely chopped
60 g / 2 oz (1 cup) finely chopped fresh coriander leaves
15 ml / 1 tbsp ground black pepper
15 ml / 1 tbsp sea salt
1.25 ml / ¼ tsp saffron threads
5 ml / 1 tsp ground ginger
2.5 ml / ½ tsp ground cumin
2.5 ml / ½ tsp sweet paprika

In a bowl, mix together all the marinade ingredients. Prick the chicken pieces with a fork or the sharp tip of a knife. Rub the marinade all over the chicken, cover with cling film (plastic wrap) and refrigerate for about 4 hours or overnight.

Heat the oil and fry the chicken pieces for about 3 minutes, until sealed. Add the onions, tomato and 300 ml / ½ pint (1¼ cups) hot water and cook, covered for 30 minutes over a moderately-low heat, turning the chicken from time to time to make sure it is covered in the juices. Meanwhile, either stone (pit) the olives and cut them in half, or leave whole. Cut the preserved lemons in half, discard the pulp and cut the rind into .6 cm / ¼ inch slices.

Add the olives, preserved lemon rind and lemon juice to the chicken and cook for a further 10-15 minutes, until the chicken is very tender and the sauce is thickened. Adjust the seasoning if necessary. (At this stage, you could turn off the heat and reheat just before you are ready to serve.) To serve, place the chicken on a warmed platter,cover completely with the olives, lemons and sauce and serve at once, either with plain couscous or boiled rice.

PRESERVED LEMONS

*I*f there is one ingredient that is indispensable to Moroccan cookery, it is preserved lemons. In the *souks* you see huge mounds of them sold loose or in preserving jars, lined up by the dozens. Their unique pickled flavour gives countless Moroccan dishes a most individual taste. I have never come across them elsewhere, and so make my own. This is extremely simple to do, but you must remember to wait a month before being tempted to use them. It is important to use ripe, smooth, thin-skinned lemons, rather than the thick-skinned variety. The peel is the part most commonly used in cooking plus the juices from the pulp.

4-6 ripe lemons
70 g/2½ oz (⅔ cup) coarse sea salt
2 x 5 cm/2 inch cinnamon sticks
6 cloves
6-8 coriander seeds
4 black peppercorns
2 bay leaves
juice of 1 lemon

To soften the peel, soak the lemons in lukewarm water for 2-3 days, changing the water daily. Drain the lemons and, using a sharp knife, cut into quarters, leaving 10 mm/½ inch of skin and flesh attached at the top and bottom. Sprinkle salt on the exposed flesh, then reshape and arrange the lemons in a preserving jar, pressing them down to release their juices and layering with more salt and the spices. Finally add the strained lemon juice to cover, leaving some space between the lemons and the lid of the jar. Cover tightly and place the jar in a warm spot, shaking the jar daily for the first ten days to distribute the spices and juice evenly.

To use, rinse the lemons as needed under cold running water. Cut the pulp away from the peel (squeezing the juice to use in the recipe) and discard the pulp. Don't worry if a white film forms on the preserved lemons in the jar; just rinse it off before using the lemons.

There is no need to refrigerate the lemons after opening. They will keep for up to a year.

WARM AUBERGINE &
SWEET RED PEPPER SALAD

*T*his makes a delicious vegetable dish served warm with chicken or fish, or cold as a starter. I have made it for parties as one of several dishes as it is easy to make in advance.

SERVES 4-6

450 g / 1 lb aubergines (eggplant)
salt
3 sweet red pepper
60 ml / 4 tbsp sunflower oil
3 cloves garlic, finely chopped
7.5 ml / 1½ tsp ground cumin
pinch of cayenne pepper
freshly ground black pepper
30 ml / 2 tbsp chopped flat leaf parsley

Cut the aubergines into thick slices. Sprinkle with plenty of salt and leave to drain in a colander for about 30 minutes. Rinse well and pat dry with absorbent kitchen paper (paper towels). Cut each slice into quarters. Meanwhile, put the peppers on a baking tray (cookie sheet) into a hot oven 200°C / 400°F / Mark 6 or under the grill (broiler) for about 30 minutes, turning from time to time, until blistered and blackened on all sides. Take the peppers out of the oven, put into a bowl, cover with a tea cloth and leave to cool for about 30 minutes.
Heat 15ml / 1tbsp of the oil in a saucepan and fry the aubergines in batches until just golden on both sides. Remove from the pan with a slotted spoon and place onto absorbent kitchen paper (paper towels) to absorb the excess oil. Continue until all the aubergines are done, adding oil to the pan as necessary. When the peppers are cool enough to handle, slip off their skins, cut each one in half, core and seed. Cut into thin strips.
Put the aubergines, peppers, garlic, cumin and cayenne pepper in a saucepan over a moderate heat, season to taste and cook gently for about 5 minutes, stirring occasionally, taking care that the aubergines do not get mushy. Serve warm or cool. Garnish with parsley.

TAJINE WITH CARDOONS & LAMB

*T*he first time I saw cardoons was in the market in Essouira, where their abundance made it obvious that in autumn they are really in season. Cardoons taste very much like artichoke hearts and look like celery, with their long stems and spiky leaves of a silvery-green colour, and they are well worth trying to find. A friend actually grows them in England quite successfully, even though they are mostly found in Mediterranean countries.

Preparing cardoons in a *tajine* is traditional in Morocco. This dish was first made for me by Amina, a cook with whom I was often seen in the kitchen at the Villa Maroc, furiously making notes as she worked with great joy and ease, and through whom I learned some of the secrets of Moroccan cooking.

Make sure the cardoons are really fresh and crisp. Fresh celery can be used instead of cardoons.

SERVES 4-6

1.4 kg/3 lb fresh cardoons
60 ml/4 tbsp olive oil
4 cloves garlic, finely chopped
1 medium Spanish onion, chopped
1.1 kg/2½ lb lamb, cut into 1½ inch chunks
1 beefsteak tomato, skinned and finely chopped
45 ml/3 tbsp chopped flat parsley

30 ml/2 tbsp chopped fresh coriander
2.5 ml/½ tsp saffron powder
5 ml/1 tsp salt
5 ml/1 tsp ground black pepper
1 small preserved lemon (Page 84)
75 g/2½ (1½ cups) green olives, rinsed and pitted
60 ml/4 tbsp lemon juice

Clean the cardoons, separate the stalks, removing any tough outer stalks and the spiky leaves. Wash well. As with celery, cardoons have long strings which can be annoying if left in the cooking, so remove them with a paring knife and cut into 7.5 cm/3 inch lengths. Place in a bowl of water and add a squeeze of lemon juice to prevent discolouration. Put the cardoons into a deep saucepan with enough salted water to cover. Bring to the boil, cover and simmer for about 40 minutes. Drain and set aside. Meanwhile, in a large casserole, heat the olive oil and fry the garlic, onion, lamb, tomato, parsley, coriander, spices and salt. Add 270 ml/9 fl oz water and bring to the boil. Reduce the heat, cover and simmer over a moderate heat for 1 hour, stirring from time to time and adding water if necessary. Add the cardoons to the casserole and continue cooking for 30 minutes, adding the preserved lemon and olives during the last 10 minutes of the cooking time. Stir in the lemon juice, one tablespoonful at a time and check for seasoning. Simmer the casserole gently, uncovered, to reduce the sauce and allow the flavours to blend.

To serve, place the lamb in a shallow serving dish and cover with the cardoons and sauce.

MARKET IN ESSOURA

CHICKEN COUSCOUS WITH SEVEN VEGETABLES

*T*here are a huge variety of couscous dishes, prepared with lamb or chicken and a multitude of different vegetables. You could try this recipe with whatever combination of fresh vegetables are in season, such as pumpkin and carrots, or courgettes (zucchini) and aubergines. Sometimes I adapt this without the chicken as a vegetable dish with couscous or rice that has been cooked with mint or coriander.

SERVES 6

60 g/2 oz (¼ cup) dried chick peas, soaked overnight, or 125 g/4 oz (1¼ cups) tinned chick peas

30 g/1 oz (2 tbsp) butter

15 ml/1 tbsp olive oil

4 chicken breasts, cut into small pieces

2 medium-sized onions, quartered

pinch of saffron threads

2.5 ml/½ tsp ground cinnamon

2.5 ml/½ tsp ground turmeric

2 dried red chillies (chilli peppers) left whole (optional)

2 cloves garlic, finely chopped

4 ripe tomatoes, skinned, seeded and quartered or 225 g/8oz (1 cup) tinned tomatoes

3 sprigs fresh coriander leaves and 4 sprigs flat leaf parsley tied together

15 ml/1 tbsp salt

5 ml/1 tsp ground black pepper

1.8 litres/3 pints (2 quarts) water

450 g/1 lb carrots, peeled

450 g/1 lb courgettes (zucchini)

225 g/½ lb turnips, peeled

450 g/1 lb pumpkin, rind removed

450 g/1 lb uncooked fine-grain couscous

handful of raisins

knob of butter

1 tsp Harissa paste

For the glazed onion sauce:

2 large Spanish onions

125 g/4 oz (1 scant cup) raisins

pinch of saffron threads

1.25 ml/¼ tsp ground turmeric

2.5 ml ½ tsp ground ginger

7.5 ml/1½ tsp ground cinnamon

60 g/2 oz (¼ cup) granulated sugar

45 g/1½ oz (3 tbsp) butter

Drain the dried chick peas and put in a pan with cold water to cover. Bring to the boil, cover and cook over a low heat for 1 hour. Drain, cool and remove the skins by gently rubbing between the fingers. If using tinned chick peas, drain and set aside.

In a heavy cast iron or other flameproof casserole, heat the butter and oil and lightly brown the chicken pieces. Add the onions, saffron, cinnamon, turmeric, chillies, garlic, tomatoes, coriander and parsley, salt and pepper. Cover and cook over a low heat for 10 minutes. Add the water and chick peas (if using tinned chick peas, add only 30 minutes before serving), bring to the boil, reduce the heat and simmer, covered, for 1 hour. Meanwhile, prepare the vegetables: cut the carrots, courgettes and turnips into quarters lengthways, then into 5 cm/2 inch lengths; cut the pumpkin into 1 inch cubes.

Begin to prepare the glazed onion topping: cut the onions into .6 cm/¹/₄ inch thick crescents. After the chicken has been cooking for about 30 minutes, transfer 450 ml/³/₄ pint (1 pint) of the simmering stock to a saucepan. Add the onions, raisins, saffron, turmeric, ginger, cinnamon, sugar, butter, salt and pepper. Cook over a moderate heat, covered for 1 hour, remove cover and continue cooking for a further 30 minutes, or until the liquid has almost evaporated and the onions have a glazed appearance. Take care not to let the mixture dry out as it may burn. Set aside, uncovered.

Put the couscous into a large bowl and pour 600 ml/1 pint (2¹/₂ cups) hot salted water over it. Leave to stand for 10 minutes, then fluff with a fork.

After the chicken has been cooking for 1 hour, add the carrots and turnips and continue cooking for 30 minutes.

Make the *Harissa* sauce: transfer 300 ml/¹/₂ pint (1¹/₄ cups) of the stock into a clean saucepan. Combine with the Harissa paste, and keep warm. To the chicken, add the courgettes, pumpkin, tinned chick peas, if using and raisins. Bring to the boil. Place the couscous in a steamer lined with a tea towel over but not submerged in the chicken mixture, cover and steam for approximately 5-10 minutes, until the couscous is done and the pumpkin is just tender. Meanwhile, reheat the glazed onion sauce. Stir a little butter into the couscous with a fork.

For the final assembly: turn the couscous onto a large heated platter. Make a well in the centre and spoon the vegetables and chicken into the well with a slotted spoon. Add some of the *Harissa* sauce, placing the remainder in a bowl to pass separately. Arrange the glazed onion sauce on top or serve in a separate bowl.

ORANGE & CARROT DESSERT

SERVES 4-6

450 g/1 lb carrots, peeled and very finely grated

1 orange, peeled, segmented and halved

juice of ¹/₂ orange

5 ml/1 tsp ground cinnamon

30-45 ml/2-3 tbsp lemon juice

15 ml/1 tbsp granulated sugar

8 dates, stoned (pitted) and chopped

yoghurt *or* double cream to serve

Mix the carrots and orange segments with the orange juice, cinnamon, lemon juice and sugar and chill, covered, in the refrigerator. Before serving, drain partially, sprinkle the chopped dates on top and serve on dessert plates, with a dash of yoghurt or double cream.

THAILAND

Markets

*T*he markets of Thailand are scented, filled with the aromas of lemon grass, rich green Kaffir lime leaves, bunches of fresh coriander (cilantro), galangal, ginger and chillies in splendid fiery reds and deepest greens.

In Bangkok, I visited the Pak Klong Talat market at the foot of the Memorial Bridge. Here, boats laden with vegetables, fruits and flowers are unloaded on the docks with fresh produce from the nearby countryside. These treasures are then snapped up by restaurateurs, shopkeepers and the general public from the early hours of the morning until late at night. Much of the produce also arrives by trucks piled high with cabbages, banana flowers, baby sweetcorn and numerous varieties of aubergines, durian, mangoes and pineapples. Hard-working porters transport huge wicker baskets filled with these exotic items and manipulate their trolleys with amazing dexterity and ease, winding their way along the narrow paths of this vast market.

The buzzing activity surrounding the fresh produce was quite bewildering. I passed a family busily sorting tall green asparagus, tying them into neat bunches and weighing each carefully. I saw the tiniest pea aubergines, large, sinister-looking bamboo shoots (looking to me more like a prehistoric ingredient!), large pumpkins, pinky-yellow small cherry tomatoes, small cucumbers and a huge variety of leaf vegetables,

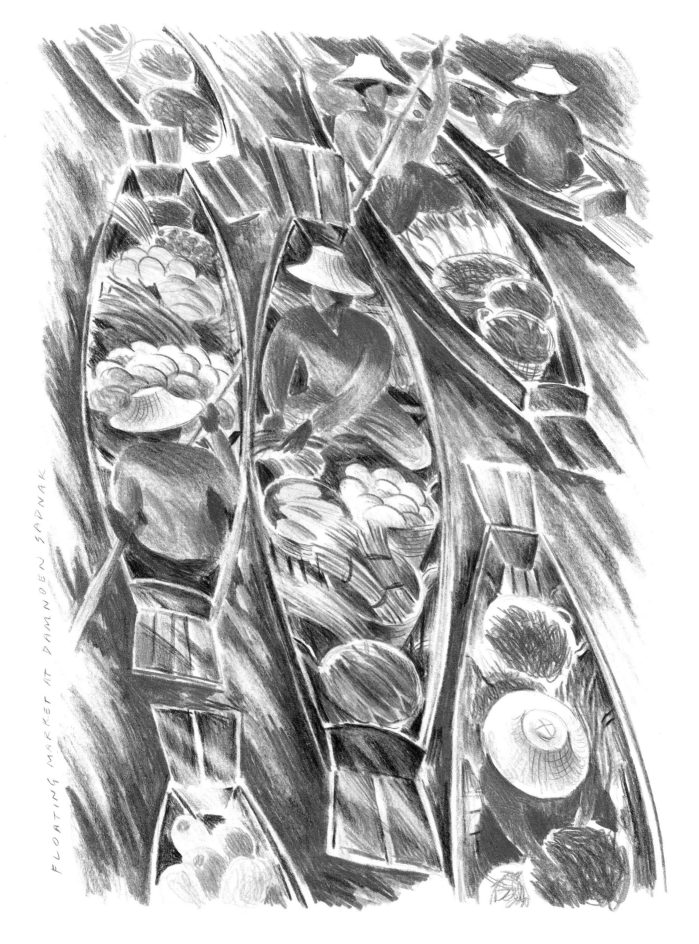

FLOATING MARKET AT DAMNOEN SADUAK

including water spinach (also known as swamp cabbage), which has spindly branches and small pointed leaves, *bok choi*, (spinach-like leaves), and many more. The variety of goods also included fried locusts and beetles; perhaps a more acquired taste!

In the midst of the covered market, a beautiful gilded shrine catches a shaft of light and gives an air of tranquillity to an otherwise noisy, busy scene. As I walked on, I passed a stall selling many varieties of chillies (a vital Thai ingredient), which mother and daughter were sorting into large, flat wicker trays, removing their stems and creating spectacular fiery red, orange and green mountains. The ease with which they handled these stinging vegetables left me wondering what their hands felt like at the end of a long day. The next stall displayed piles of galangal, a younger, hotter type of ginger root; light pink and green in colouring and delicious used thinly sliced in soups. Lemon grass, probably one of the most important ingredients in Thai cooking, lay beside bunches of holy basil, somewhat sweeter, yet spicier than the better-known Italian basil and used to give a real zest to curries. The strong fish smells emanating from shops selling shrimp paste and fish sauce in vast bowls was less alluring to my nose, but these ingredients are also vital in Thai cooking.

Like many others in Thailand, this market stays open most of the night; a new phenomenon, so that many housewives who now work during the day can shop for their evening meal. With husbands and children in tow, they search out bunches of fresh *bok choi*, baby green aubergines, lemon grass and chillies. They stop to buy freshly fried prawn and spinach fritters, barbecued bananas or the juiciest mangoes; delicious served with sticky rice or perhaps, durian fruit. One stop will certainly be at the flower market, where orchids of lightest pinks and deepest reds are sold for almost nothing and where women sit at tables preparing ornate garlands of richly perfumed flowers.

After sketching and taking notes of these exotic ingredients one whole afternoon, my appetite was aroused and I couldn't resist sitting down at one of the many outdoor stalls preparing local food to enjoy a delicious Tom Yam Gung, (prawn and mushroom soup). The combination of spices, lemon grass and ginger were all splendid; also the crunchiness of vegetables that had been cooked for the shortest possible time. The separate taste of every combined ingredient, which to me is what makes Thai food so exciting and enjoyable, really came through.

MIXED VEGETABLE CURRY

A typical Thai dinner almost always includes some type of curry and a soup. This is a particularly tasty vegetable curry. If you wish to serve it to vegetarian guests, you will have to eliminate the shrimp paste from the red curry paste when preparing it.

SERVES 4-6

45 ml/3 tbsp vegetable oil
30 ml/2 tbsp red curry paste, (page 96)
390 ml/13 fl oz coconut milk
115 g/4 oz (¾ cup) bamboo shoots, roughly chopped
115 g/4 oz baby sweetcorn, halved lengthways
115 g/4 oz Chinese long beans or fine green beans cut into 2.5 cm/1 inch lengths
115 g/4 oz small green aubergines (eggplant) halved or regular aubergines cut into small dice

115 g/4 oz cauliflower, cut into small florets
30 ml/2 tbsp light soy sauce
10 ml/2 tsp sea salt
10 ml/2 tsp sugar
8 whole Kaffir lime leaves
3 large fresh hot red chillies, cut into thin slices
25 holy basil or sweet basil leaves
30 ml/2 tbsp ground roasted peanuts
30 ml/2 tbsp finely-chopped fresh coriander (cilantro) leaves

Heat the oil in a wok or large frying pan over a moderate heat. Briefly fry the curry paste, add the coconut milk and stir well. Add all the remaining ingredients, stir-frying until the vegetables are just tender, but still crisp. Serve sprinkled with coriander leaves.

CURRY PASTES

*A*n essential ingredient in Thai cooking, green or red curry pastes are often available ready-made, but making your own is a bit like making your own Italian pesto sauce: there is something very satisfying in making something from scratch and using the freshest ingredients. Use a pestle and mortar or blender.

You will save considerable time when producing a meal if you make these pastes in advance. They may then be stored in an airtight container in the refrigerator for several weeks.

GREEN CURRY PASTE
Makes 1 175 ml / 6 fl oz jar

6 hot green chillies with seeds, chopped
2 shallots, peeled and roughly chopped
4 cloves garlic, peeled
4 cm / 1½ inch knob fresh galangal, chopped
4 fresh coriander (cilantro) roots
2 stalks fresh lemon grass, thinly sliced
5 ml / 1 tsp finely chopped Kaffir lime leaves
10 black peppercorns
2.5 ml / ½ tsp coriander seeds
1.25 ml / ¼ tsp cumin seeds
10 ml / 2 tsp shrimp paste
75 ml / 5 tbsp coconut or vegetable oil

Put the chillies, shallots, garlic, galangal, coriander root and lemon grass in a mortar or blender. Pound or blend slightly, then add the lime leaves, peppercorns, coriander and cumin seeds and shrimp paste and blend until smooth. Finally, incorporate the oil, blending thoroughly.

RED CURRY PASTE
Makes 1 175 ml / 6 fl oz jar

2 dried red chillies
2 shallots, peeled and roughly chopped
4 cloves garlic, peeled
2 cm / ¾ inch knob fresh galangal, chopped
2 cm / ¾ inch root ginger, chopped
2 coriander (cilantro) roots, chopped
2 stalks lemon grass, finely sliced
10 ml / 2 tsp finely chopped Kaffir lime leaves
10 black peppercorns
1.25 ml / ¼ tsp coriander seeds
1.25 ml / ¼ tsp cumin seeds
1.25 ml / ¼ tsp ground cinnamon
5 ml / 1 tsp ground turmeric
1 tsp sea salt
10 ml / 2 tsp shrimp paste
75 ml / 5 tbsp vegetable oil

Soak the dried chillies in warm water for at least 20 minutes, until soft. Drain and chop and place in a mortar or blender with the shallots, garlic, galangal, ginger, coriander root and lemon grass. Pound or blend slightly, then add the lime leaves, peppercorns, coriander and cumin seeds, cinnamon, turmeric, salt and shrimp paste and blend until smooth. Finally, incorporate the oil, blending thoroughly.

LEMON GRASS

THAI BASIL

SALANGAL

CORIANDER ROOT

GINGER

SHALLOTS

KAFFIR LIME LEAVES

HOT CHILLIES

THAI CHILLIES

CHICKEN, MUSHROOM & COCONUT SOUP

*T*his is one of the most popular of all Thai soups, flavoured with lemon grass and galangal. When I enjoyed a delicious supper at the new Sakothai Hotel in Bangkok, this soup was served in half a coconut shell and looked wonderful. When coconuts are cheap in the market, I now do the same!

SERVES 4-6

6 cloves garlic, roughly chopped
3 shallots, peeled and roughly chopped
5 ml / 1 tsp finely-chopped coriander (cilantro) root
2 stalks lemon grass, finely sliced
8 peppercorns
5 ml / 1 tsp red curry paste, (page 96)
2 cm / ³/₄ inch knob fresh galangal, finely sliced
390 ml / 13 fl oz coconut milk

225 g / 8 oz boneless chicken breast, finely sliced
390 g / 14 oz straw mushrooms
210 ml / 7 fl oz vegetable stock
45 ml / 3 tbsp fish sauce (*nam pla*)
45 ml / 3 tbsp fresh lime juice
2 fresh hot green chillies, finely chopped
5 ml / 1 tsp finely chopped Kaffir lime leaves
chopped coriander (cilantro) leaves

Put the garlic, shallots, coriander root, lemon grass, peppercorns, curry paste and half the galangal in a mortar and pound until smooth, or process in a blender with a little of the coconut milk.

Pour half the coconut milk into a medium-sized saucepan and bring to the boil over a moderate heat. Add the blended spice paste and heat for 4-5 minutes, then add the chicken, remaining galangal, mushrooms and coconut milk and stock and return to the boil. Reduce the heat and allow to simmer until the chicken is tender, about 2 minutes, then add the fish sauce, lime juice, chillies and lime leaves. Cook, stirring for a further minute, then remove from the heat and serve in small bowls, garnished with coriander leaves.

FARMS OUTSIDE CHIANG MAI

CAULIFLOWER & COCONUT SOUP

Vatcharin Bhumichitr has become one of the authorities on Thai cooking in Britain and when I visited his Chiang Mai restaurant in London, I so enjoyed this soup, he kindly shared his recipe with me In Thailand, vegetables are cooked for only a short time so that they remain crunchy.

SERVES 4

120 ml / 4 fl oz coconut milk
2 stalks lemon grass, finely sliced
2 cm / ³⁄₄ inch knob fresh galangal, finely chopped
5 Kaffir lime leaves, roughly chopped into quarters
30 ml / 2 tbsp light soy sauce

5 ml / 1 tsp sugar
720 ml / 24 fl oz vegetable stock
1 small cauliflower, cut into florets
2 fresh small red or green chillies, finely chopped
30 ml / 2 tbsp fresh lemon juice
coriander (cilantro) leaves

In a large saucepan over a moderate heat, bring the coconut milk, lemon grass, galangal, lime leaves, soy sauce, sugar, vegetable stock and cauliflower to a boil. Reduce the heat and simmer until the cauliflower is cooked, but still crisp. Remove from the heat and add the chillies and lemon juice. Stir, pour into small individual soup bowls and garnish with coriander leaves.

OYSTER MUSHROOM SOUP

This is the simplest of soups, full of the flavour of the Orient. Oyster mushrooms, with their delicate taste are perfect in this elegant soup.

SERVES 4

720 ml / 24 fl oz vegetable stock
2 stalks lemon grass, finely sliced
5 ml / 1 tsp finely chopped Kaffir lime leaves
30 ml / 2 tbsp light soy sauce
5 ml / 1 tsp sugar
30 ml / 2 tbsp fresh lime juice
55 g / 2 oz (1 cup) coarsely chopped oyster mushrooms
1 fresh red or green chilli, finely chopped
chopped coriander (cilantro) leaves
spice

In a large saucepan over a moderate heat, bring the vegetable stock to the boil. Add all the remaining ingredients, except the garnish and stir well until the mushrooms are just cooked. Pour into small individual bowls and garnish with coriander leaves.

SPRING ROLLS

*T*here is nothing quite as satisfying, in my opinion, as hot, freshly-made thin and crispy spring rolls. Here are recipes for two fillings and two sauces suitable for spring rolls, to be served either with drinks or as a starter. Spring roll pastry sheets (wonton wrappers) and cellophane noodles made from mung bean paste are available at Oriental food shops.

MAKES 24 SPRING ROLLS

Mushroom, Carrot and Prawn filling

100 g / 3½ oz cellophane noodles, soaked and finely chopped

55 g / 2 oz (1 cup) dried wood ear mushrooms, soaked and finely chopped

55 g / 2 oz (½ cup) bean sprouts

55 g / 2 oz (½ cup) freshly-grated carrots

115 g / 4 oz (1 cup) cooked prawns (shrimp), chopped

15 g / 1 tbsp light soy sauce

15 g / 1 tbsp finely-chopped garlic

2.5 ml / ½ tsp-ground black pepper

5 ml / 1 tsp salt

1.25 cm / ½ inch root ginger, peeled and finely chopped

Sweet Potato and Onion filling

2 cloves garlic, roughly chopped

5 ml / 1 tsp coriander (cilantro) root, finely chopped

5 ml / 1 tsp whole black peppercorns

30 ml / 2 tbsp vegetable oil

85 g / 3 oz (⅔ cup) sweet potato, finely diced

85 g / 3 oz (⅔ cup) carrots, finely diced

85 g / 3 oz (½ cup) onions, finely chopped

85 g / 3 oz baby sweetcorn, chopped

15 ml / 1 tbsp light soy sauce

5 ml / 1 tsp sugar

Chilli Sauce

60 ml / 4 tbsp rice vinegar or fresh lime juice

30 ml / 2 tbsp water

15 ml / 1 tbsp sugar

3 hot red chillies, finely sliced

Coconut Sauce

15 ml / 1 tbsp groundnut oil

1 small onion, peeled and finely chopped

5 cm / 2 inch (thick end) stalk lemon grass, finely sliced

5 ml / 1 tsp ground coriander seeds

85 g / 3 oz creamed coconut

approximately 45 ml / 3 tbsp vegetable stock

For the spring roll pastry:

6 large spring roll (wonton wrapper) pastry sheets 18 cms / 7 in square

5 ml / 1 tsp cornflour (cornstarch)

vegetable oil for deep-frying

First make the filling of your choice. To make the mushroom filling, place all the ingredients in a large mixing bowl and stir well. Set aside. To make the sweet potato filling, place the garlic, coriander root and peppercorns in a mortar or blender and process into a paste, using a little water if necessary. Heat the oil in a medium-sized saucepan over a moderate heat and fry the spice paste for 1 minute. Add the rest of the ingredients and cook, stirring constantly for 3-4 minutes. Set aside.

Next, make the sauces. To make the chilli sauce, simply mix all of the ingredients together. To make the coconut sauce, fry the onion lemon grass and coriander in the oil until the mixture is fragrant. Stir in the coconut cream. When it has melted, remove from the heat and add enough stock to give it a good dipping consistency.

Assemble the spring rolls as close to serving as possible, otherwise the pastry will get soggy and won't fry well.

Cut the spring roll pastry sheets to make squares of approximately 9 cm/3½ inches. Add a little cold water to the cornflour to make a paste. Place a little filling on each square, one at a time, brush the uncovered edges with the cornflour paste, then start to roll up, bringing in the edges to enclose the filling well and press the edges to close.

To deep-fry, heat the oil in a wok or deep-fryer to a temperature of 180°C/350°F/Mark 4 or until a cube of white bread turns golden in 1 minute. Slip the rolls into the hot oil, approximately six at a time and deep-fry until golden-brown. Remove with a slotted spoon and drain on absorbent kitchen paper (paper towels).

If you wish to deep-fry the rolls in advance, do not over-fry them, reheat in a hot oven for 5 minutes or re-fry in hot oil for 1 minute, immediately before serving.

STIR-FRIED ASPARAGUS, CORN AND PRAWNS

I enjoyed this superbly tasty stir-fry at one of the many open-air restaurants and stalls at the Pak Klong Talat market in Bangkok, watching the chef quickly prepare all the vegetables in an enormous wok over an equally enormous flame!

SERVES 4

30 ml / 2 tbsp vegetable oil
3 cloves garlic, finely chopped
200 g / 7 oz thin asparagus, cut into 2.5 cm / 1 inch lengths
115 g / 4 oz baby sweetcorn
15 ml / 1 tbsp dark soy sauce
60 ml / 4 tbsp vegetable stock
1 ripe tomato, finely chopped
5 ml / 1 tsp plain white flour

115 g / 4 oz large cooked prawns sliced lengthways
1 large carrot, peeled and cut into matchsticks
2.5 cm / 1 inch root ginger, peeled and cut into fine matchsticks
2.5 ml / ½ tsp chilli powder
55 g / 2 oz fresh water spinach, *bok choi* or fresh spinach

Heat the oil in a wok or frying pan over a moderate heat and add the garlic. Fry until golden-brown. Add the asparagus stalks (reserving the tips for later) and baby corn and stir-fry for 2-3 minutes. Stir in the soy sauce, vegetable stock and tomato. Add the flour and stir until thickened slightly. Add the prawns, carrots, asparagus tips, ginger and chilli powder and stir-fry for a further 2 minutes. Finally, add the water spinach, *bok choi or* spinach, cook for 1 minute, remove from the heat and serve immediately.

MUSHROOM & BROCCOLI STIR-FRY

*A*nother lovely, fresh, quick vegetable stir-fry, using dried mushrooms.

SERVES 4

55 g/2 oz dried Chinese mushrooms
30 ml/2 tbsp vegetable oil
3 cloves garlic, finely chopped
170 g/6 oz (1½ cups) broccoli stems, cut
 lengthways into thin slices
15 ml/1 tbsp light soy sauce
5 ml/1 tsp dark soy sauce
60 ml/4 tbsp vegetable stock
1 tomato, skinned and finely chopped
5 ml/1 tsp plain white flour
2.5 cm/1 inch root ginger, peeled and cut
 into fine matchsticks
2.5 ml/½ tsp chilli powder

Cut the mushrooms in half, remove stems. Soak in warm water for
30 minutes.
Heat the oil in a wok or large frying pan over a moderate heat and fry
the garlic until golden-brown. Add the drained mushrooms and broccoli
and briefly stir-fry. Add the light and dark soy sauce, vegetable stock and
tomato. Stir. Stir in the flour, ginger and chilli powder. Serve hot.

BROCCOLI IN OYSTER SAUCE

*T*his dish is a variation of a classic Chinese Vegetable in Oyster Sauce
dish that uses a kale-type vegetable.

SERVES 4

450 g/1 lb broccoli
30 ml/2 tbsp vegetable oil
2 cloves garlic, finely chopped
60 ml/4 tbsp oyster sauce
10 ml/2 tsp light soy sauce
sea salt and freshly-ground black pepper

Divide the broccoli into florets. Reserve the stems for Mushroom &
Broccoli Stir-Fry (above).
Place the broccoli florets in a steamer over rapidly boiling water and
cook for 3-4 minutes, until just tender. Drain and refresh in cold water to
retain the colour.
Heat the oil in a wok or frying pan over a moderate heat and fry the
garlic until golden-brown, then add the broccoli, oyster sauce and soy
sauce and stir fry for 2-3 minutes. Remove from the heat, season to taste
and transfer to a serving dish.

THE PAK KLONG TALAT MARKET. BANGKOK

HOT & SOUR SOUP WITH STRAW MUSHROOMS & PRAWNS

*S*oups are an essential part of a Thai meal and are normally eaten together with rice and the other dishes of the meal. However, one often sees women in the markets preparing different varieties of soups to be enjoyed on their own as a filling snack. I prefer to serve Thai soups as a starter as our tradition is to use soup to set the scene for the dishes to follow.

This soup does need to have a kick to it, so leave the seeds in the chillies. Coriander root is one of the important ingredients in Thai cooking, and can be bought as part of fresh coriander bunches. Also use King prawns or the largest prawns you can find.

SERVES 4-6

7 peppercorns
5 ml / 1 tsp finely-chopped coriander (cilantro) root
300 ml / 10 fl oz vegetable stock
1 stalk lemon grass, cut into 2.5 ml / ¹⁄₂inch lengths (only use the lower third)
2.5 cm / 1inch knob fresh galangal, chopped
5 ml / 1 tsp finely chopped Kaffir lime leaves

45 ml / 3 tbsp fresh lemon juice
45 ml / 3 tbsp fish sauce (*nam pla*)
1-2 small hot red chillies, finely chopped
2.5 ml / ¹⁄₂ tsp sugar
390 g / 14 oz tinned straw mushrooms, halved
450 g / 1 lb raw king prawns, peeled (except for tail shell) and deveined
chopped coriander (cilantro) leaves

In a mortar, pound the peppercorns and coriander root to make a paste or process in a blender with a little of the stock. Heat in a medium-sized saucepan over a moderate heat with the stock, stirring well. Add the lemon grass, galangal, lime leaves, lemon juice, fish sauce, chillies and sugar. Bring to the boil and simmer for 3 minutes. Add the mushrooms and prawns and cook for a further 2-3 minutes until the prawns are cooked through. Serve in small bowls garnished with coriander leaves. If you prefer, you can prepare the soup in advance, adding the prawns and mushrooms just before serving.

GREEN AUBERGINE CURRY

*T*he baby green aubergines seen in the markets of Thailand are ideal for this dish and are available in most Oriental food shops. However, if you cannot find them, normal-sized purple aubergines (eggplant) may be substituted. I serve this curry with rice to absorb the juices.

SERVES 4

240 ml / 8 fl oz thick coconut milk

30 ml / 2 tbsp vegetable oil

2 cloves garlic, finely chopped

45 ml / 3 tbsp green curry paste, (page 96)

30 ml / 2 tbsp bottled fish sauce (*nam pla*)

15 ml / 1 tbsp palm or brown sugar

340 g / 12 oz baby green aubergines (eggplant) or purple aubergine, cut into bite-sized pieces

4 Kaffir lime leaves, roughly torn into quarters

15 holy or sweet basil leaves

2 fresh red chillies, seeded and cut into strips

In a small saucepan over a low heat, gently heat the coconut milk. Do not allow to boil.

Put the oil into a wok or frying pan over a moderate heat. Add the garlic and fry until golden-brown. Add the curry paste and stir-fry for a few seconds. Add the coconut milk, stirring, until it starts to bubble. Add the fish sauce and sugar and cook for 3-4 minutes. Stir in the aubergines and Kaffir lime leaves and cook for a further 8 minutes, until the aubergines are just tender. Add the basil leaves and chillies. Remove from the heat and serve immediately with boiled rice.

PAD THAI NOODLES

*A*nyone who has travelled to Thailand has probably enjoyed this dish in one of its many variations, always freshly-prepared in a wok. You can prepare all the ingredients in advance, but you must leave the frying until just before serving.

SERVES 4

115 g/4 oz *sen lek* noodles
60 ml/4 tbsp groundnut or vegetable oil
2 cloves garlic, finely chopped
12 large fresh cooked prawns, shelled and deveined
1 egg, beaten
30 ml/2 tbsp lemon juice
30 ml/2 tbsp fish sauce (*nam pla*)
2.5 ml/½ tsp brown sugar
30 ml/1 oz (3 tbsp) roasted peanuts, roughly chopped

30 ml/2 tbsp coarsely-ground dried shrimp
2.5 ml/½ tsp chilli powder
15 ml/1 tbsp preserved turnip, freshly chopped (optional)
30 ml/1 oz (¼ cup) beansprouts
4 spring onions (scallions), sliced into 2.5 cm/1 inch lengths
30 ml/2 tbsp finely-chopped fresh coriander (cilantro) leaves to garnish
lime wedges to garnish

Cover the noodles with cold water in a bowl and soak for 20 minutes, until soft. Drain and set aside.

Pour the oil into a wok or large frying pan over a moderate heat, add the garlic and prawns, if using, and fry until golden-brown.

Working quickly, stir the egg into the wok for a few seconds, until it separates into threads. Add the noodles and stir well. Add the lemon juice, fish sauce, sugar, half the peanuts, dried shrimp, chilli powder, turnips, if using, beansprouts and spring onions, stir-frying for a few minutes. Remove from the heat and serve garnished with the remaining peanuts, coriander leaves and lime wedges.

NOODLES WITH BROCCOLI STEMS AND LONG BEANS

*I*n Thailand, every part of a leaf vegetable is used; in this case, the stems, which are as important as the florets and leaves.
Fresh white *sen yai* noodles are available from Oriental food shops.

SERVES 4

115 g/4 oz fresh white *sen yai* noodles
240 ml/8 fl oz coconut milk
15 ml/1 tbsp red curry paste, (page 96)
5 ml/1 tsp sea salt
5 ml/1 tsp sugar
15 ml/1 tbsp tamarind juice (optional)
85 g/3 oz (³/₄ cup) beansprouts
115 g/4 oz long beans or fine green beans,
   cut into 2.5 cm/1 inch lengths
115 g/4 oz (1 cup) broccoli stems, peeled
   and cut thinly across
45 g/1¹/₂ oz (¹/₃ cup) whole roasted peanuts

First blanch the noodles in a large pan of boiling water for 2-3 minutes. Remove from the heat, drain, refresh under cold water and set aside. In a wok or large frying pan, gently heat the coconut milk over a low heat. Stir in the curry paste and mix well. Add the salt, sugar and tamarind juice, if using and cook for 2 minutes. Add the beansprouts, beans and broccoli stems and cook for a further 2-3 minutes. Add the noodles, mix well and cook for a further 2 minutes. Remove from the heat and serve, garnished with the whole roasted peanuts.

SPICY QUICK-FRIED LONG BEANS

*I*n the Pak Klong Talat market of Bangkok, I saw men and women sitting cross-legged on the floor, sorting yard-long beans and arranging them in neat bundles for shoppers.

This is a quick and easy dish to prepare which leaves the beans deliciously crunchy. If long beans are not available, substitute fine green beans. Ready-fried beancurd is sold in most Oriental food shops.

SERVES 4

30 ml / 2 tbsp vegetable oil

5 ml / 1 tsp finely-chopped garlic

15 ml / 1 tbsp red curry paste, (page 96)

225 g / 8 oz Chinese long beans or fine green
   beans, cut into 2.5 cm / 1 inch lengths

30 ml / 2 tbsp light soy sauce

60 ml / 4 tbsp vegetable stock

5 ml / 1 tsp sugar

30 ml / 2 tbsp ground roast peanuts

5 ml / 1 tsp finely chopped Kaffir lime leaves

85 g / 3 oz (¾ cup) ready-fried beancurd,
   finely sliced

Heat the oil in a wok or large frying pan and fry the garlic until golden-brown. Stir in the red curry paste, then add the long beans, soy sauce, vegetable stock, sugar, peanuts, Kaffir lime leaves and beancurd. Stir-fry gently until heated through. Serve immediately.

WOMEN SORTING YARD LONG BEANS BANGKOK

GREEN PAPAYA SALAD

When I visited the market in Mai Tang near Chiang Mai in northern Thailand, I spotted a woman making this delightful salad. Using a huge pestle and mortar, she added the ingredients one by one, making sure they were well mashed. After grating the papaya, she mixed everything together and sold the salad together with succulent barbecued chicken. People queued for this speciality at lunchtime and after I tried it, I could see why. The chilli and fish sauce blend with the tart crispness of the green papaya in a combination of flavours that is marvellous with other traditional Thai dishes.

SERVES 4

115 g/4 oz (½ small) raw green papaya
2 small garlic cloves, finely chopped
30 ml/2 tbsp roasted peanuts, roughly ground
2 medium-sized green or red chillies, finely chopped
30 ml/2 tbsp fish sauce (*nam pla*)
30 ml/2 tbsp lemon juice
15 ml/1 tbsp dried shrimp, roughly ground
20 ml/4 tsp palm or brown sugar
1 medium-sized tomato, thinly sliced
115 g/4 oz long beans or fine green beans, cut into 2.5 cm/1 inch lengths
peel of ½ lime, finely sliced

Peel the papaya and grate, using a hand grater to get the longest possible strands.

With a pestle and mortar, pound the garlic, half the peanuts, chillies, fish sauce, lemon juice, shrimp and sugar, adding one ingredient at a time and mix well. Alternatively, process in a blender or food processor. Turn into a bowl. Add the tomato, beans, lime peel and grated papaya and toss well.

To serve, turn into a serving dish lined with banana leaf if available and mound the salad on top. Garnish with the remaining peanuts.

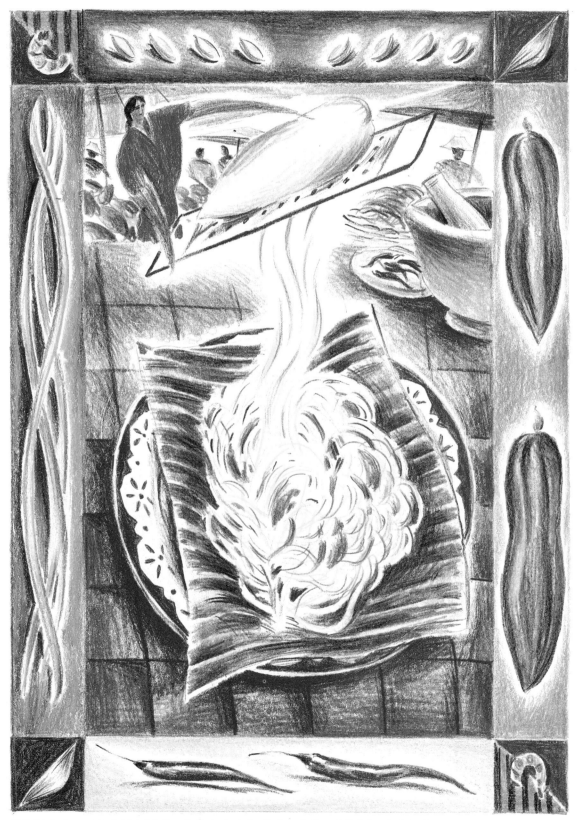

WOMAN MAKING PAPAYA SALAD · MAI TANG

POTATO & ONION CURRY

*A*part from the mildness of this curry, its great asset is that it can be prepared in advance and reheated just before serving. Normally made with chicken or beef, I find it can be just as delicious without meat of any kind. Other vegetables, such as cauliflower, carrots and beans can be added to make a more substantial vegetable curry.

SERVES 4

240 ml / 8 fl oz thick coconut milk

30 ml / 2 tbsp vegetable oil

2 cloves garlic, finely chopped

15 ml / 1 tbsp red curry paste, (page 96)

45 ml / 3 tbsp fish sauce (*nam pla*)

5 ml / 1 tsp sugar

30 ml / 2 tbsp lemon juice

240 ml / 8 fl oz vegetable stock or water

280 g / 10 oz small potatoes, peeled and quartered

280 g / 10 oz medium-sized onions, peeled and quartered

225 g / 8 oz (1½ cups) chicken breast, chopped (optional)

45 ml / 3 tbsp roasted peanuts, roughly chopped

In a small saucepan over a low heat, gently heat the coconut milk. Do not allow to boil.

Put the oil into a wok or frying pan over a moderate heat. Add the garlic and fry until golden-brown. Add the curry paste and stir-fry for a few seconds. Add the warmed coconut milk, stirring, until it starts to bubble. Add the fish sauce and sugar and cook for 3-4 minutes. Add the lemon juice, vegetable stock, potatoes, onions and chicken and simmer for 10 minutes over a moderate heat. Add 30 ml / 2 tbsp of the peanuts and cook for a further 4-5 minutes.

To serve, turn into a warmed serving dish and garnish with the remaining peanuts.

FARMERS PICKING BEANS

WINGED BEAN SALAD

*D*uring my stay at the Royal Orchid Hotel in Bangkok, this spicy salad became one of my favourite dishes at the Thara Thong restaurant. Winged beans, also called asparagus pea or dimbala, have deep, ruffled ridges that stand out like wings and are wonderfully crunchy. They are available in Oriental food shops, but you may substitute stringless green beans.

SERVES 4-6

150 g / 5 oz winged beans, thinly sliced
  across

3 small fresh hot green chillies

1 fresh hot red chilli

85 g / 3 oz roasted peanuts

115 g / 4 oz (1 cup) large prawns,
  cooked and cut in half

85 g / 3 oz (³/₄ cup) chicken breast,
  cooked and shredded

85 g / 3 oz creamed coconut

30 ml / 2 tbsp fish sauce (*nam pla*)

45 ml / 3 tbsp fresh lime juice

30 ml / 2 tbsp sugar

3 shallots, peeled and sliced

15 ml / 1 tbsp coconut milk

Blanch the winged beans rapidly in boiling water, drain and plunge into cold water to retain the colour and crisp texture.
Pound the chillies and peanuts with a pestle and mortar and place in a large bowl. Add the prawns, chicken, creamed coconut, fish sauce, lime juice and sugar. Mix well. Add the winged beans and shallots and toss to incorporate. Transfer to a serving dish and sprinkle the coconut milk on top.

INDIAN
Markets

*T*he magic and spirit of India is something you can really begin to experience when visiting any of the innumerable street markets. India is a country full of colour, vitality, ancient traditions, beautiful people, bewildering landscapes, the highest snowcapped mountains in the north and vast fields of coconut trees in the south. It also possesses a cooking tradition that has been in existence for hundreds of years, influenced by its rulers as well as its climate. Many Indians follow a strict vegetarian diet, so they have explored numerous delicious ways of preparing vegetables.

In Delhi, I visited several local markets in the old city and the feeling, as you get off your rickshaw, leaving traffic, noise, fumes and the madness of every-day life behind and find yourself in the narrow paths where little seems to have changed since the middle ages, is quite wonderful. Such tranquillity leaves one free to admire, select and purchase marvellous produce.

Indian women in long, flowing saris of deepest red and orange-yellow, do the serious task of shopping with great pride and joy, selecting okra with utmost care, one by one, making sure they are all young and tender. Only the smoothest, firm, deep-mauve aubergines will do. They pick just the right-sized fresh hot green chillies, a basketful of red onions or turnips, bitter gourds, small yellowish cucumbers and an assortment of red or yellow juicy, ripe tomatoes. Bunches of fresh coriander *methi*, small bunches of spinach and the tiniest garlic cloves are also essentials. A sacred cow or two happily roams the narrow paths, everyone respecting their presence.

In the market of Sabji Mande, numerous stalls are shaded by worn sacking cloth that extends over the streets, managing to exclude the hot sun for most of the day. Here the men, who are very much the workers, pull the horsedrawn carts into place and unload fresh produce. They look rather elegant in their white cotton baggy trousers

MARKET STALL IN DELHI

and brightly-coloured shirts, setting up at sunrise and staying open for business late into the evening.

I was lured to a small stall where the owner was busy grinding fresh spices, such as cumin, coriander, cardamom and cinnamon to make fresh *garam masala*, page 121, an indispensable ingredient in Indian cooking. The aroma left me quite entranced, as did the sight of huge orange, red and sienna-coloured pyramids of these exotic spices carefully displayed. Spices are essential in Indian cooking; their variety is vast, yet with only a few selected ones, a dish can be transformed into a really memorable meal.

My interest in seeing where the healthy produce sold at market came from, led me to visit the countryside north of Delhi, filled with vast expanses of agricultural land and farmers who still work the land as their forefathers did. On the way, I saw tiny, lively roadside markets, huge camels and ancient-looking water buffalo, that are still used in farming.

I asked my taxi driver to stop when I saw a huge field of cauliflowers and aubergines, growing amongst tiny mud-built farmhouses and as I walked along a narrow path, I found myself in a field of bright green chillies. I couldn't resist cutting off a small bunch, which I later dried and brought back to London! I met the entire family of farmers, cousins, aunts and uncles, grandparents and, of course, the water buffaloes. The young farmer plucked fresh onions out of the rich, dark soil as a gift for me. Their warmth left me filled with delight that these people still do their work with such pleasure, harmony and respect for the earth.

In Madras, the streets that lead to the main covered market are filled with peasant women in colorful saris, selling the ripest, red plum tomatoes or ginger carefully arranged in pyramids on top of colourful fabric laid out on the pavement as if it were an offering to the gods. A few stalls offer delicious snacks, such as *chhole*, a popular chick pea curry, (page 126), attracting a hungry queue. I couldn't forgo trying some and stood on the pavement, enjoying it and watching rickshaws, bicycles and the colorful crowds busily going about their day's work.

GARAM MASALA

*T*his spice mixture is a vital ingredient in Indian cooking and I have used it in a number of recipes throughout this section. It is best made in small quantities at a time (as in this recipe), so that it is always fresh and truly aromatic.

MAKES ABOUT 90ML/6TBSP

30 ml/2 tbsp cardamom seeds
10 cm/4 inch cinnamon stick
10 ml/2 tsp cumin seeds
10 ml/2 tsp whole cloves
10 ml/2 tsp black peppercorns
5 ml/1 tsp freshly-grated nutmeg

Place all the ingredients in an electric coffee-grinder or mini blender. Process for 40-50 seconds until the spices are finely ground. Store in an airtight jar in a cool place, away from direct sunlight.

AUBERGINES IN YOGHURT SAUCE

*I*n India, aubergines are often peeled before use, giving a different appearance to the finished dish. This is a mild and creamy recipe, with a rich yellow colour.

SERVES 4

450 g/1 lb aubergines (eggplant)
45 ml/3 tbsp vegetable oil
2 large onions, finely chopped
3 cloves garlic, crushed
2.5 cm/1 inch root ginger, finely chopped
5 ml/1 tsp ground coriander
2.5 ml/1/2 tsp ground turmeric
2.5 ml/1/2 tsp chilli powder
5 ml/1 tsp salt
5 ml/1 tsp sugar
60 ml/4 tbsp water
240 ml/8 fl oz yoghurt

Preheat the oven to 200°C/400°F/Mark 4. Put the aubergines on a baking tray and bake for about 30 minutes, or until tender. Leave to cool, then peel and remove the stalk. Chop the aubergine flesh finely.
Heat the oil in a saucepan over a moderate heat and fry the onions until they become transparent. Add the garlic and ginger. Stir well. Add the coriander, turmeric, chilli, salt, sugar and water. Stir well and reduce the heat to low. Simmer gently, covered, for 3 minutes.
Mix in the chopped aubergines. Cover the pan and simmer gently for 5 minutes. Mix in the yoghurt a little at a time. Heat through and serve immediately.

VEGETABLE SAMOSAS

*S*amosas make a delicious appetizer served with drinks, or a main course served with rice and salad. This is one of the classic fillings. The bonus is that any leftover filling can be reheated and served as a potato dish at another meal.

Making one's own samosas can be time-consuming, but their freshness and crisp texture makes it worthwhile.

MAKES 16 SAMOSAS

For the pastry:

225 g/8 oz (2 cups) plain white flour
2.5 ml/¹⁄₂ tsp salt
2.5 ml/¹⁄₂ tsp ground cumin
60 ml/4 tbsp vegetable oil
60 ml/4 tbsp iced water

For the filling:

15 ml/1 tbsp vegetable oil
5 ml/1 tsp cumin seeds
5 ml/1 tsp black mustard seeds
1 medium-sized onion, finely chopped
140 g/5 oz (1 cup) shelled fresh or defrosted frozen peas
2.5 cm/1 inch root ginger, peeled and finely grated

1-2 fresh hot green chilli peppers, finely chopped
15 ml/1 tbsp finely-chopped coriander leaves (cilantro)
45 ml/3 tbsp water
1 medium-sized potato, boiled, peeled and cut into small dice
5 ml/1 tsp sea salt
5 ml/1 tsp ground coriander
5 ml/1 tsp *garam masala,* (page 121)
5 ml/1 tsp ground cumin
1.25 ml/¹⁄₄ tsp cayenne pepper
30 ml/2 tbsp lemon juice
vegetable oil for deep-frying

Sift the flour, salt and cumin together in a large bowl. Add the oil and rub in with the fingers until the mixture resembles coarse breadcrumbs. Slowly add the water and gather the dough into a stiff ball. If the dough won't hold together, add another spoonful of water. Turn the dough out onto a floured work surface and knead for 5 minutes, until smooth. Re-form into a ball. Rub with a little vegetable oil, slip the dough into a plastic bag and refrigerate for 30 minutes.

Make the filling. Heat the oil in a wok or large frying pan over a moderate heat. Add the mustard and cumin seeds and fry until they begin to pop. Add the onion and stir-fry until golden-brown at the edges. Add the peas, ginger, chilli peppers, coriander leaves and water. Cover, reduce the heat and simmer until the peas are cooked, stirring occasionally and adding a little water to the pan if the mixture appears to be drying out. Add the potatoes, salt, ground coriander, garam masala, cumin, cayenne pepper and lemon juice. Stir to mix. Cook over a low heat for 3-4 minutes, stirring gently. Remove from the heat and allow the filling to cool.

Take the dough from the refrigerator and knead again. Divide into 8 portions. Roll each portion into a 20 cm/8inch round, keeping the

FRESH SAMOSAS IN DELHI MARKET

remaining portions covered. Using a pastry cutter or saucer, cut out a circle 17.5 cm / 7 inches in diameter and cut in half with a sharp pointed knife. Pick up one semicircle and form a cone, making a wide, overlapping seam. Seal with a little water. Fill each cone with about 30 ml / 2 tbsp filling. Close the top of the cone by sealing the edges together with a little water. Make the rest of the samosas in the same way. Pour enough vegetable oil to half-fill a wok or large frying pan. Heat to 180°C / 350°F / Mark 4, or until a cube of white bread turns golden in 1 minute. Slide about 3 or 4 samosas into the hot oil and fry slowly, turning them frequently, until they are golden-brown and crisp. Drain on absorbent kitchen paper (kitchen towels). Serve hot or warm.

ONION & COURGETTE BHAJIS

*W*hen you see these delectable *bhajis* being freshly fried in huge woks in open-air stalls throughout India, or in restaurants, the temptation is to order more than you can really eat. They make a marvellous starter, served with mango chutney or cucumber and mint raita. You can prepare them in advance, giving them an initial fry and then refry them for a minute or two or just reheat in a hot oven (200°C / 400°F / Gas 6) for 5-7 minutes.

SERVES 4-6

10 ml / 2 tsp cumin seeds
10 ml / 2 tsp coriander seeds
2 fresh green chillies, finely chopped
3 cloves garlic, crushed
1 cm / ½ inch root ginger, peeled and grated
225 g / 8 oz (2 cups) chickpea flour *or* plain white flour
5 ml / 1 tsp ground turmeric
2 large onions, finely sliced and then chopped

450 g / 1 lb courgettes (zucchini), coarsely grated
2.5 ml / ½ tsp *garam masala*, (page 121)
5 ml / 1 tsp salt
45-60 ml / 3-4 tbsp iced water
oil for deep-frying
1 lemon, cut into wedges to garnish

Grind the cumin and coriander with a mortar and pestle or in an electric spice or coffee grinder. In a large bowl, combine the chillies, garlic, ginger, cumin, coriander, flour, turmeric, onions, courgettes, *garam masala* and salt. Stir in enough of the water to give a soft dropping consistency.
Heat the oil in a deep-fryer or wok to 180°C / 350°F / Mark 4 (until it is hot enough to turn a cube of bread golden in 1 minute). Take a generous spoonful of the mixture and drop into the hot oil. Cook about 3-4 at the same time until golden-brown. Remove with a slotted spoon and drain on absorbent kitchen paper (paper towels). Continue until you have used up all the batter. Serve hot with mango chutney or cucumber and mint raita (page 132), garnished with the lemon wedges.

SPICED SMALL AUBERGINES

Small aubergines are to be seen everywhere in the markets of India and Indian housewives certainly make good use of them. You can substitute ordinary aubergines, cutting them into 1.25 cm / ½ inch slices, but the smaller ones are worth searching out since they are available in many Oriental shops.

SERVES 4-6

5 ml / 1 tsp sesame seeds
5 ml / 1 tsp coriander seeds
5 ml / 1 tsp poppy seeds
2 dried red chillies, roughly chopped
5 cm / 2 inch piece root ginger, peeled and finely chopped
4 cloves garlic, crushed
15 ml / 1 tbsp roughly-chopped fresh coriander leaves (cilantro)

2 fresh green chillies
6 curry leaves
280 g / 10 oz small aubergines (eggplant)
60 ml / 4 tbsp vegetable oil
2.5 ml / ½ tsp cumin seeds
15 ml / 1 tbsp tamarind paste
salt to taste

Grind the sesame seeds, coriander seeds, poppy seeds and dried red chillies in a coffee grinder or pound with a pestle and mortar. Set aside. Mix the ginger, garlic, coriander leaves, one of the green chillies and curry leaves in a blender or food processor. Mix with the ground spices to form a paste.

Make two deep cuts along the length of the aubergines, leaving the four sections held together by the stem and base. Rub a little of the spice paste into each aubergine and set the remainder aside. Cut the remaining chilli into thin strips and deseed if wished.

Heat the oil in a wok or large saucepan over a moderately high heat and fry the cumin seeds for a few seconds, until they begin to pop. Add the chilli strips and fry for 1 minute. Add the remaining spice paste and cook, stirring occasionally, until the oil has separated, about 3-4 minutes. Add the aubergines and simmer, covered, reducing the heat to moderate until the aubergines are nearly cooked, about 15 minutes, stirring occasionally.

Mix the tamarind paste with 60 ml / 4 tbsp hot water and mix well. Add the tamarind mixture to the aubergines and stir gently. Simmer until the aubergines are cooked and serve hot.

This dish can be prepared in advance and reheated.

CHICKPEAS WITH TOMATO CURRY

*I*n the narrow streets of old Delhi, near Chandri Chowk, a district of cloth traders, where women sit happily for hours choosing suitable fabrics for their saris, men with small portable carts set themselves up and sell *chhole*, a delicious chickpea curry served on small green leaves. It is a perfect snack. The mixture is kept hot in a large brass bowl and chopped coriander is ready to be sprinkled on top with slices of lime to garnish. I like to serve this dish with plain rice or *nan*, a type of Indian bread.

SERVES 4

225 g/8 of dried chickpeas
4 cloves garlic, crushed
60 ml/4 tbsp vegetable oil
2 medium-sized onions, finely chopped
2 small green chilies, seeded and finely chopped
5 ml/1 tsp ground turmeric
5 ml/1 tsp paprika
15 ml/1 tbsp ground cumin

5 ml/1 tsp ground coriander
5 ml/1 tsp *garam masala* (page 121)
4 medium tomatoes, seeded and chopped
30 ml/2 tbsp chopped coriander leaves (cilantro)
1 ml/1 tbsp chopped mint
salt and freshly-ground black pepper
fresh chopped coriander (cilantro)

Soak the chickpeas overnight. Drain and place in a large saucepan with half the garlic. Cover with plenty of fresh water, bring to the boil, reduce the heat, cover and simmer for 2-3 hours, until tender. Drain well and set aside.

Heat the oil in a heavy-based saucepan. Add the remaining garlic and chopped onions and fry gently for about 5 minutes, until soft and lightly coloured. Add the chillies, turmeric, paprika, ground cumin, coriander and *garam masala* and fry, stirring, for a further 1-2 minutes. Add the tomatoes, coriander and mint and cook gently, stirring, for 5-10 minutes, until the tomatoes turn into a puree. Add the chickpeas and stir well. Simmer gently for a further 5 minutes, until the chickpeas are heated through. Add salt and pepper, remove from the heat and turn into a warmed serving dish. Serve hot, garnished with fresh chopped coriander.

CHHOLE BEING SOLD IN CHANDRI CHOWK

SPICED PUMPKIN SOUP

*H*uge pumpkins were displayed in the markets of Madras, where I saw
local traders come early to bargain for the best price, having inspected
the produce with great care. My Indian friends prepared this delicious
soup for me and its subtle taste and elegant colour makes it ideal
for entertaining.

SERVES 6

30 ml/2 tbsp vegetable oil
1 medium-sized onion, chopped
1.25 cm/¹/₂inch root ginger, chopped
670 g/1¹/₂ lb pumpkin, rind removed,
  seeded and chopped
450 ml/³/₄ pint (2 cups) chicken or
  vegetable stock

¹/₂ cinnamon stick
150 ml/5 fl oz milk
salt and freshly-ground black pepper
30 ml/2 tbsp lime juice
a few coriander (cilantro) leaves

Heat the oil in a large saucepan over a low heat. Add the onion and
ginger and cook very gently for 2-3 minutes, stirring constantly. Add the
pumpkin, chicken or vegetable stock and cinnamon. Increase the heat
and bring to the boil, then reduce the heat and simmer until the pumpkin
is very soft, about 15-20 minutes. Remove from the heat. Remove the
cinnamon stick and purée the soup in a blender or food processor.
Return the soup to the rinsed-out saucepan over a moderate heat. Add
the milk and salt and pepper to taste and bring to the simmering point.
Remove from the heat, add the lime juice and serve immediately,
garnished with a few coriander leaves.

SWEET POTATO WITH ONIONS

*T*he sweet potato is a wonderful vegetable, which is generally under-used. Its natural sweetness is a real contrast to the spices in this recipe.

SERVES 4
670 g / 1½ lbs sweet potatoes
45 ml / 3 tbsp vegetable oil
5 ml / 1 tsp black mustard seeds
5 ml / 1 tsp cumin seeds
3 large onions, thinly sliced
2.5 ml / ½ tsp chilli powder
5 ml / 1 tsp *garam masala*, (page 121)
5 ml / 1 tsp freshly-squeezed lemon juice
15 ml / 1 tbsp chopped fresh coriander leaves
   (cilantro) to garnish

Wash the sweet potatoes and put them, unpeeled, into a large saucepan of boiling water and cook for 15-20 minutes, until tender. Drain and leave to cool in a colander.
Meanwhile, heat the oil in a saucepan over a moderate heat. When hot, add the mustard seeds and cumin seeds. As soon as they begin to pop, add the onions and fry until golden-brown, stirring occasionally.
Stir in the chilli powder and *garam masala* and simmer gently for a few minutes.
Meanwhile, peel the potatoes and cut in half lengthways, then into .5 cm / ¼ inch slices. Add to the onion mixture, sprinkle with lemon juice and cook over a very high heat until the sweet potatoes begin to brown, about 3-5 minutes. Remove from the heat.
Serve on a warmed dish, garnished with chopped coriander.

MIXED VEGETABLE CURRY

A really hearty curry, this makes a complete meal served with warm
nan bread and Cucumber & Mint Raita, (page 132).

SERVES 6

1 kg / 2 lb potatoes

450 g / 1 lb cauliflower, broken into
  florets

250 g / 8 oz French beans (green
  beans), trimmed and cut into 2.5
  cm / 1 inch lengths

30 ml / 2 tbsp vegetable oil

5 ml / 1 tsp black mustard seeds

5 ml / 1 tsp coriander seeds

5 ml / 1 tsp cumin seeds

5 ml / 1 tsp ground turmeric

5 ml / 1 tsp chilli powder

2.5 ml / $^{1}/_{2}$ tsp ground cardamom

30 ml / 2 tbsp freshly-squeezed lemon
  juice

150 ml / 5 fl oz water

salt and freshly-ground black pepper

115 g / 4 oz ($^{3}/_{4}$ cup) fresh or defrosted
  frozen peas

4 medium-sized tomatoes, skinned
  and cut into quarters

30 ml / 2 tbsp finely-chopped
  coriander leaves (cilantro)

Peel the potatoes and cut into large chunks. Cook in boiling salted water
for about 8 minutes, until just tender. Drain and set aside.
Cook the cauliflower and beans in boiling salted water for 5 minutes.
Drain and set aside.
Heat the oil in a large saucepan. Add the mustard, coriander and cumin
seeds and fry, covered, for 2 minutes. (The mustard seeds will pop when
they become hot). Add the potatoes, cauliflower, beans, turmeric and
chilli powder, tossing the vegetables over a high heat for 2 minutes. Add
the lemon juice, water, salt and pepper to taste and peas. Mix together
well, cover, reduce the heat to low and cook for 10 minutes. Add the
tomatoes and coriander leaves and cook for a further 5 minutes. Remove
from the heat and serve immediately.

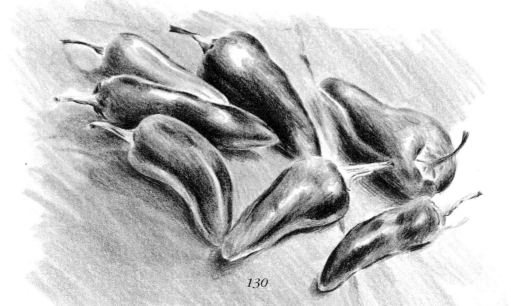

AUBERGINE WITH TOMATOES

A very popular, mild dish, use small aubergines if available. This is very good served with Chicken Korma with Spinach, (page 138) and Potatoes & Spinach, (page 135).

SERVES 4-6
90 ml/6 tbsp vegetable oil
4 cloves garlic, crushed
1 large onion, thinly sliced
2 fresh green chillies, thinly sliced
800 g/1¾ lb aubergines, thinly sliced
5 ml/1 tsp ground cumin
pinch of ground turmeric
2.5 ml/½ tsp cayenne pepper
400 g/14 oz tinned tomatoes with juice
salt
30 ml/2 tbsp chopped coriander (cilantro)

Heat the vegetable oil in a large saucepan over a moderate heat. Add the garlic and onion and fry until the onions are transparent and just turning golden. Add the chillies and fry for a further minute. Add the aubergines, stir well and simmer for 5 minutes, stirring occasionally. Add the cumin, turmeric, cayenne pepper, tomatoes, salt to taste and stir well. Simmer, covered, for 15 minutes. Correct seasoning if necessary.
Serve in a warmed serving bowl, sprinkled with coriander.

CUCUMBER & MINT RAITA

*N*o Indian meal is ever complete without this clean-tasting, cooling raita, which soothes the palate when eating spicy food. An interesting variation is to substitute mooli for the cucumber, or use a combination of the two vegetables.

SERVES 4
360 ml/12 fl oz plain yoghurt
½ medium-sized cucumber, peeled,
   coarsely grated and drained
30 ml/2 tbsp finely-chopped fresh mint
5 ml/1 tsp ground cumin
2.5 ml/½ tsp ground coriander
5 ml/1 tsp salt
pinch of paprika
4 fresh mint leaves to garnish

Pour the yoghurt into a bowl and beat lightly with a fork or whisk until smooth and creamy. Add the remaining ingredients and mix well. Cover and refrigerate until needed. To serve, garnish with mint leaves.

GIRLS IN TRIVANDRUM · KERALA

PANEER

*P*aneer is a nutritious type of home-made cheese, used in a variety of vegetarian dishes throughout India. It is simple to make and will keep in the refrigerator for up to 2 days.

MAKES APPROX. 350 G / 12 OZ
2 litres / 3½ pints (2 quarts) full fat milk
60 ml / 4 tbsp freshly-squeezed lemon juice

Heat the milk slowly in a large, heavy-based saucepan over a low heat and bring to the boil. Remove from the heat and gradually stir in the lemon juice. Continue to stir gently until the milk curdles. Set aside and allow to cool for a few minutes.
Meanwhile, line a sieve with a piece of muslin or a clean tea towel and hang over a bowl. Pour the curdled milk into the sieve and leave to drain for 1 hour. The paneer will now be quite solid.
For pressed paneer, leave the cheese in the muslin, place on a flat work surface, cover with a plate and weight down for at least 1 hour. Cut into cubes or use as directed in the following recipes.

SPICY PANEER WITH OKRA

*T*his is a dry and spicy dish, perfect served with Chicken Korma (page 137) and basmati rice, or even as a starter.

SERVES 4

280 g / 10 oz fresh young okra
75 ml / 5 tbsp vegetable oil
5 ml / 1 tsp cumin seeds
2.5 cm / 1 inch root ginger, peeled and finely chopped
3-4 fresh green chillies
1 medium-sized onion, finely chopped

5 ml / 1 tsp turmeric
280 g / 10 oz paneer (page 134), cut into 1.25 cm / ½ inch cubes
5 ml / 1 tsp chilli powder
salt
30 ml / 2 tbsp water
15 ml / 1 tbsp chopped coriander leaves (cilantro) to garnish

Wash the okra and pat dry. Top and tail and cut into thin slices. Heat 45 ml / 3 tbsp vegetable oil in a saucepan over a moderate heat and stir-fry the okra until just brown. Remove from the pan with a slotted spoon and set aside.
Add the remaining oil to the saucepan and when hot, add the cumin seeds and fry until they start to pop. Add the ginger and green chillies and stir. Add the onion and fry until golden-brown. Add the turmeric and stir well. Add the paneer to the pan and fry for 3-4 minutes. Add the okra, chilli powder, salt to taste, and water and simmer over a low heat for 5 minutes. Remove from the heat.
To serve, turn into a warmed serving dish. The chillies can be removed before serving if wished.

POTATOES & SPINACH

*T*his is a very mild dish with a lovely, subtle taste. Potatoes are a staple in India, as is spinach, and you will find this combination in numerous parts of the country.

SERVES 4-6

900 g / 2 lb fresh spinach
75 ml / 5 tbsp vegetable oil
10 ml / 2 tsp black mustard seeds
1 large onion, thinly sliced
2 cloves garlic, finely chopped

450 g / 1 lb potatoes, peeled and cut
   into 2 cm / ³/₄ inch cubes
1.25 ml / ¹/₄ tsp cayenne pepper
2.5 ml / ¹/₂ tsp ground coriander
5 ml / 1 tsp salt
30 ml / 2 tbsp water

Wash the spinach thoroughly and put into a large saucepan with only the water clinging to the leaves. Cook gently over a moderate heat until the spinach has wilted. Remove from the heat and drain in a colander, pressing out as much of the liquid as possible. Chop roughly.
Heat the oil in a heavy saucepan over a moderate heat. When hot, add the mustard seeds. As soon as they begin to pop, add the onion and garlic. Stir-fry for 2 minutes. Add the potatoes, cayenne pepper and coriander. Stir-fry for a further 2 minutes. Add the spinach, salt and water. Bring to the boil. Cover tightly, reduce the heat to very low and cook gently for 35 minutes, until the potatoes are tender, stirring occasionally and making sure there is always some liquid in the pan.
When the potatoes are tender, remove from the heat, turn into a warmed serving dish and serve immediately.

OKRA WITH ONIONS

Okra, also known as "ladies fingers" or *bhindi*, is used extensively in curries, with fish, stuffed, stewed and stir-fried. Choose small, young tender okra for best results and avoid those with dark blemishes.

SERVES 4-6

450 g / 1 lb fresh young okra
5 cloves garlic, peeled
2.5 cm / 1 inch root ginger, peeled and
  roughly chopped
120 ml / 4 fl oz water
16 ml / 4 tbsp vegetable oil
5 ml / 1 tsp cumin seeds
1 large onion, thinly sliced

5 ml / 1 tsp ground turmeric
10 ml / 2 tsp ground cumin
5 ml / 1 tsp chilli powder
5 ml / 1 tsp salt
10 ml / 2 tsp freshly-squeezed lemon
  juice
15 ml / 1 tbsp chopped fresh coriander
  leaves (cilantro)

Wash the okra and pat dry. Top and tail and cut into 1.25 cm / ½ inch pieces. Set aside. Put the garlic, ginger and 45 ml / 3 tbsp of the water into a blender and purée.

Heat the oil in a frying pan over a moderate heat. Add the cumin seeds and as soon as they begin to pop, add the garlic puree and stir-fry for 1 minute. Add the onion and cook until golden-brown, about 5 minutes.

Add the turmeric, ground cumin, chilli powder, salt, lemon juice and remaining water. Mix well. Stir in the okra, cover, reduce the heat to low and simmer for about 10 minutes, until the okra is tender.

To serve, garnish with chopped coriander leaves.

CHICKEN KORMA WITH SPINACH

*T*his exquisite dish is deliciously perfumed with an array of subtle spices and is not at all "hot". The whole spices remain in the dish when served, so just take care to pick them out as you go (and warn your guests). It is a perfect main course dish for entertaining as it can be prepared in advance and reheated just before serving. You can also omit the cream and use double the amount of yoghurt if you prefer.

SERVES 4-6

450 g / 1 lb fresh spinach

75 ml / 5 tbsp vegetable oil

2 large onions, thinly sliced

4 large black cardamom pods, crushed

12 whole cloves

5 ml / 1 tsp black peppercorns

6 green cardamom pods, crushed

2 x 7.5 cm / 3 inch cinnamon sticks

10 whole almonds

2 bay leaves

6 boneless, skinless chicken breasts, cut into bite-sized cubes

600 ml / 1 pint (2½ cups) plain yoghurt

600 ml / 1 pint (2½ cups) double (heavy) cream

2.5 ml / ½ tsp ground turmeric

2.5 ml / ½ tsp chilli powder

6 cloves garlic, peeled and crushed

2.5 cm / 1 inch root ginger, peeled and finely grated

1.25 ml / ¼ tsp freshly-grated nutmeg

salt and freshly-ground black pepper

Wash the spinach and put in a large pan with just the water clinging to its leaves. Cook over a gentle heat until just wilted. Remove from the heat, drain well and set aside.

Heat the vegetable oil in a large frying pan and fry the onions until golden-brown and crisp. Remove from the pan with a slotted spoon and leave to drain on absorbent kitchen paper (paper towels).

Add the black cardamom, cloves, peppercorns, green cardamom, cinnamon, almonds and bay leaves to the oil in the pan and fry for 1 minute. Add the chicken pieces to the pan and stir-fry for 3-4 minutes. Remove the chicken pieces from the pan with a slotted spoon, leaving the spices behind, and place on kitchen paper to drain.

Chop the onions finely or process in a blender or food processor and add to the spices.

Lightly whisk the yoghurt and cream together and add with the turmeric and chilli powder to the pan. Mix well and simmer, covered, over a low heat, for 5 minutes.

Add the garlic, ginger, nutmeg and chicken to the pan and stir well. Add salt and pepper to taste. Continue to simmer, covered for 15 minutes, checking from time to time to make sure the mixture does not boil.

Meanwhile, chop the spinach. Add the spinach to the pan, cover and cook for a further 5 minutes over a low heat. Remove from the heat, turn into a warmed serving dish and serve immediately.

TURNIPS WITH TOMATOES AND MINT

*J*aipur in Rajasthan is the home of the famous Hawa Mahal Palace of the Winds; a pink sandstone building encrusted with fine jali work and balconies. It is here that the palace women watched the street life below where today there is a vegetable market. Mounds of mauve and white turnips grown in the nearby fields make their way to this market and look splendid, sold by sari-clad women.

SERVES 6

670 g / 1½ lb turnips
60 ml / 4 tbsp vegetable oil
340 g / 12 oz tomatoes, skinned and roughly chopped
2.5 cm / 1 inch root ginger, peeled and finely grated
15 ml / 1 tbsp ground coriander
2.5 ml / ½ tsp ground turmeric
1.25 ml / ¼ tsp cayenne pepper
450 ml / ¾ pint (2 cups) water
45 ml / 3 tbsp chopped coriander leaves (cilantro)
30 ml / 2 tbsp chopped fresh mint leaves
5 ml / 1 tsp salt

Peel the turnips and cut in half lengthways, then cut into 1.25 cm / ¼ inch thick slices.
Heat the ghee or oil in a wok or frying pan over a moderately high heat. Add the tomatoes and stir-fry for 2 minutes. Add the ginger, ground coriander, turmeric and cayenne pepper. Stir-fry for a further 2 minutes, until the sauce is thick. Add the turnips, water, coriander and mint leaves and salt. Partly cover and cook over a moderately low heat for 20 minutes, stirring occasionally. Cover tightly and cook for a further 10 minutes over a low heat until the turnips are tender.

PEA & CORIANDER PILAF

*T*he Raintree Restaurant in Madras serves superb southern Indian food in its gardens and this is where I first tasted this pilaf. It has a subtle green colour and the cashew nuts, so popular in India, add a delicious crunch.
Serve this pilaf with Okra and Onions, (page 137) or Aubergines with Tomatoes, (page 132).

SERVES 6

170 g/6 oz (1 scant cup) basmati rice
4 whole cloves
6 cloves garlic, peeled
4-5 fresh hot green chilli peppers
seeds of 2 cardamom pods
10 ml/2 tsp coriander seeds
10 ml/2 tsp cumin seeds
2.5 cm/1 inch root ginger, peeled and roughly chopped

60 ml/4 tbsp chopped coriander leaves (cilantro)
60 ml/4 tbsp vegetable oil
115 g/4 oz cashew nuts
115 g/4 oz (¾ cup) shelled fresh or defrosted frozen peas
600 ml/1 pint (2½ cups) water
sea salt
chopped coriander leaves to garnish

Wash the rice thoroughly under cold, running water, until the water runs clear.
Process the cloves, garlic, chillies, cardamoms, coriander seeds, half the cumin seeds, ginger and coriander leaves with a little water.
Heat half the oil in a small saucepan over a moderate heat and fry the cashew nuts until golden. Remove the nuts with a slotted spoon and set aside. In the same oil, fry the processed spices for 1 minute. Add the peas and 120 ml/4 fl oz of the water and season to taste with a little salt. Cook until the peas are tender.
Meanwhile, heat the remaining oil in a medium-sized saucepan over a moderate heat and fry the remaining cumin seeds for 1 minute. Add the rice, mix and fry for 1 minute. Add the remaining water, season with salt, cover and cook over a very low heat for 15 minutes. Add the pea mixture, mix well and cook, uncovered, for 1-2 minutes to heat through.
Serve hot, garnished with chopped coriander leaves and cashew nuts.

SELLING RICE & LENTILS IN GURGAON MARKET

COURGETTES WITH PRAWNS

*T*his is a quick and easy recipe with fresh, strong tastes. Use large Pacific prawns (jumbo shrimp) if you want to make this for a special occasion.

SERVES 4

15 ml / 1 tbsp vegetable oil
2 cloves garlic, crushed
1 medium-sized onion, finely chopped
340 g / 12 oz courgettes (zucchini), cut into matchsticks
2.5 ml / ¹/₂ tsp ground turmeric
5 ml / 1 tsp ground cumin
5 ml / 1 tsp ground coriander

5 ml / 1 tsp finely grated root ginger
pinch of cayenne pepper
30 ml / 2 tbsp freshly-squeezed lemon juice
5 ml / 1 tsp salt
250 g / 8 oz peeled prawns (shrimp)
85 g / 3 oz (1¹/₂ cups) finely-chopped coriander leaves (cilantro) to garnish

Heat the oil in a wok or large frying pan over a moderate heat. Add the garlic and onions and fry until the onions are transparent. Add the courgettes, turmeric, cumin, coriander, ginger, cayenne pepper, lemon juice and salt. Stir to mix well. Add the prawns, reduce the heat to low and simmer, covered, for 3 minutes. Remove the lid, increase the heat to moderate and allow the sauce to reduce and thicken.
Serve hot, garnished with coriander leaves.

POTATOES WITH CUMIN

*T*his potato dish is a joy for anyone who enjoys cumin. I first tasted it at the Dhaba restaurant, Claridges Hotel in Delhi, which serves delicious Punjabi food.

SERVES 6

8 cloves garlic, peeled
5 cm/2 inch root ginger, peeled and
  roughly chopped
30 ml/5 tbsp water
100 ml/3½ fl oz vegetable oil
30 ml/2 tbsp cumin seeds
250 g/8 oz tomatoes, skinned and
  quartered

1 kg/2 lb potatoes, peeled and cut
  into 2 cm/¾ inch cubes
15 ml/1 tbsp ground cumin
5 ml/1 tsp sea salt
5 ml/1 tsp chilli powder
15 ml/1 tbsp chopped coriander
  leaves (cilantro)

Purée the garlic and ginger with 45 ml/3 tbsp of the water in a blender.
Heat the oil in a wok or large frying pan over a moderate heat and fry
the cumin seeds for a few seconds until they begin to change colour.
Add the garlic purée and fry for 1 minute. Add the tomatoes, potatoes,
ground cumin, salt, chilli powder and remaining water. Stir well and cook
for 15-20 minutes, stirring from time to time until the potatoes are tender,
adding a little water if the mixture becomes too dry.
Served garnished with chopped coriander.

CARROT HALVA

*T*his makes a delicious dessert and can be prepared in advance, giving
the cardamom time to infuse well into the carrot mixture. I generally
serve small portions with cream or yogurt on the side.

SERVES 6

450 g/1 lb carrots, peeled and grated
750 ml/1¼ pints (3 cups) full fat milk
8 cardamom pods
5 tbsp vegetable oil

75 ml/5 tbsp sugar
30 ml/2 tbsp sultanas (golden raisins)
30 ml/2 tbsp shelled, unsalted
  pistachio nuts, lightly crushed

Put the carrots, milk and cardamom pods in a heavy-based saucepan
over a moderate heat and bring to the boil. Reduce the heat to moderate
and cook, stirring occasionally, until all of the liquid has evaporated.
Remove from the heat.
Heat the oil in a non-stick frying pan over a moderately-low heat. Add
the carrot mixture and stir-fry until the carrots no longer have a wet,
milky appearance and turn a rich, reddish colour. This can take 10-15
minutes. Add the sugar, sultanas and pistachio nuts. Stir-fry for a further 2
minutes. Remove from the heat.
Carrot Halva can be served warm or at room temperature. Decorate each
portion with a few whole pistachio nuts or serve with cream or yogurt.

MEXICAN &
GUATEMALAN
Markets

The colour and magic of the markets of Central America are almost indescribable, with women dressed in vibrant, hand-woven textiles in the brightest reds, turquoises and mauves. They carry large wicker baskets from their farms and lay out their fresh produce on the pavement, using some of their bright textiles as a backdrop. They display firm, red tomatoes, the healthiest-looking carrots I have ever come across, basketsful of palm hearts with elegant pointed tops, a huge variety of potatoes of varying colours and shapes and giant radishes, which the market women proudly sprinkle with water to retain their vivid red colour. Large green avocados lay in glossy mounds wherever I looked. There were many vegetables I had not encountered in such profusion before, such as chayotes (a type of squash that is cooked like potatoes), yucca or cassava (a root vegetable that is delicious fried) and plantains (related to bananas, but used as vegetables), which can be made into appetizing snacks. Also on view were small, bright green tomatillos, a type of cape gooseberry used in making a spicy green sauce.

In Guatemala I visited the village of Zunil, which sits at the base of a dramatic valley with green volcanic mountains rising above the town and often hidden by low cloud. The surrounding agricultural land has such fine weather all year round with tropical rain and hot sunshine, it is the largest vegetable-producing area for Guatemala and other parts

SANTIAGO MARKET GUATEMALA

of Central America. I was astonished to see vast fields of broccoli growing profusely, as well as cauliflower, cabbage and fields of onions extending for miles into the steep land above. The roofs of the small farmhouses scattered around this valley are the perfect place to dry the corn that is the staple diet of the natives and has been since the Mayans lived here some 400 years ago. The Mayans also grew avocados, beans, potatoes, tomatoes, chillies and pumpkin, starting the vegetable traditions that are still so important in the local cooking.

In Zunil, the colourful market takes place in front of the Spanish colonial church, painted white with carved columns and an ornate doorway. People were friendly, but a little shy as I sketched, hastily trying to capture the mood and some of the details. Corn was being boiled or grilled for hungry passers-by, eaten with a spicy chilli-salt mixture. Huge barrels or canvas bags were filled with golden-yellow, white, purple or red varieties of corn, which are cooked and made into the dough used to make *tortillas*. Women were busy selling banana leaves, used for the *tamales* found all over Central America. *Tamales* are made from maize flour (*masa harina*) dough, stuffed with vegetables, seafood or pork, wrapped in a banana leaf and steamed.

In the market of Merida, northern Yucatan, limes, tomatillos and black avocados were displayed as well as the most impressive variety of fresh and dried chillies I saw anywhere. There are over 100 varieties of chillies in Mexico; the Aztecs and Mayans both used them for medicinal and culinary purposes. With the help of

Columbus and the spice trade, the chilli spread to the Far East, India and Africa, where it became an essential ingredient. Bright green and red *jalapeño* and *serrano* were the most popular and readily available fresh chillies, along with *habañeros* (also known as Scotch bonnets), used in fiery sauces. *Poblanos*, are used in stuffed and deep-fried *chiles relleños*. There were also huge, flat baskets filled with the tiniest green, yellow and red *pequin* chillies, which are probably the hottest of all. There was also an abundance of deepest brown, black and red dried chillies, which looked very much like sun-dried tomatoes, used in the famous *mole*, a nutty, spicy sauce used with turkey and vegetables. Their subtle flavours make them an important ingredient in

Mexican cooking and they are nearly always roasted, then soaked.

Women were at work peeling bean pods to reveal dark and glossy black and red kidney beans, commonly used in soups, stews and as tortilla toppings. They were delighted to offer a stranger unripe green mangoes, sliced and dipped into a chilli-salt mixture, which I ate with the hope that the chilli would not turn my mouth into an inferno. Surprisingly enough, these were quite mild and delicious. Yucatan convinced me that not all Mexican food is hot and spicy, since most dishes here have a subtle flavour. When chillies are used, dishes can either be mild or hot, according to individual preference. As I do not personally enjoy very spicy food, the recipes in this section tend to be mild to medium-hot, but extra chilli can be added by those who like "hot" food.

One of my fondest memories of visits to markets in this region was a short lunch break in Santiago, a village on the famous Lake Atlitan, after a morning of drawing and talking to local people. I stopped to buy fresh tortillas that had been deep-fried and on which a good helping of guacamole had been spread, with some finely-shredded radish and a little chilli *salsa* on top. The tortilla was so light and crisp and the topping so fresh and tasty, I soon found myself enjoying a second helping. I then carried on with the afternoon's sightseeing, totally revitalized by my snack.

Just a note of caution: try to use gloves when handling fresh chillies, since contact with any sensitive area, such as the eyes or mouth, can be most unpleasant and even dangerous. When chopping chillies, I hardly touch them, using a knife and fork so as to avoid any mishaps. Always wash the hands carefully after chopping.

YUCATAN LIME SOUP

I first tasted this soup in the town of Merida, northern Yucatan, which boasts a marvellous market with the most impressive variety of chillies I have seen anywhere. The strong, sour taste of lime that comes through in this soup and the combination of avocado and vegetables is very appealing. This simple, healthy soup makes an excellent lunch or light supper.

SERVES 4-6

15 ml / 1 tbsp olive oil

1 medium-sized red onion, finely chopped

3 cloves garlic, finely chopped

10 ml / 2 tsp dried oregano

2.5 ml / ^{1}/$_2$ tsp salt

225 g / 8 oz boneless, skinless chicken breasts (optional)

2 small carrots, peeled

225 g / 8 oz fine green beans, topped and tailed and cut into 2.5 cm / 1inch lengths

2 medium-sized ripe tomatoes, skinned, seeded and chopped

1.5 litre / 2^1/$_2$ pints (1^1/$_2$ quarts) vegetable or chicken stock

10 fresh coriander stems, tied into a bunch

5 ml / 1 tsp chilli powder

2 limes cut into thin slices

juice of one lime

1 ripe avocado, peeled and diced to garnish

10 sprigs fresh coriander to garnish

Heat the oil in a large fireproof casserole. Add the onion, garlic, oregano, salt and chicken (if using) and cook over a moderately low heat until the onion is transparent. Meanwhile, cut the carrots in half lengthways, then into 5 mm / ^{1}/$_4$inch slices. Add the carrots, beans and tomatoes to the casserole. Pour in the heated stock and the bunch of coriander and simmer for about 20 minutes.

Remove the chicken breasts from the casserole with a slotted spoon and set aside until cool enough to handle. Shred by hand into thin strips. Set aside.

Add the chilli powder and lime slices and juice to the stock. Simmer for a further 5 minutes over a moderate to low heat. Remove the bunch of coriander. Correct the seasoning if necessary, add the shredded chicken and simmer for another 5 minutes. To serve, ladle the soup into individual bowls and garnish with the diced avocado and coriander.

If you prefer a milder, more delicate lime flavour, pare the skin from 2 limes with a sharp knife, removing the white pith. Segment the flesh, chop into bite-sized pieces and add as a garnish.

MERIDA MARKET. MEXICO

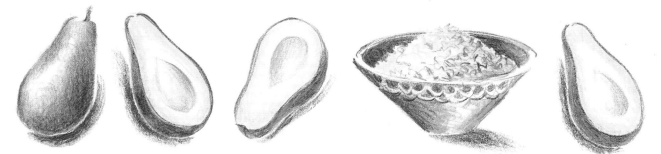

GUACAMOLE

Guacamole or avocado dip appears in many variations. I first tasted this in the market of Antigua; just mashed, ripe avocado, mixed with a little salt and lemon juice, as a tortilla topping. Delicious! A more interesting variation is the following recipe, which includes some chilli and coriander. Use as much or as little of the chilli as you feel comfortable with.

Guacamole makes a delicious dip for tortilla chips and is best served the same day you prepare it. Use ripe avocados as they are easier to mash and have a better flavour. Reserve one avocado stone (pit) and put it into the prepared mixture so that it does not discolour.

SERVES 6

2 large, ripe avocados, halved and stoned
  (pitted)
1/2 small red onion, very finely chopped
1 clove garlic, crushed
15 ml / 1 tbsp finely chopped fresh coriander
1 fresh green jalapeño chilli pepper, seeded
  and finely chopped
2 medium-sized ripe tomatoes, peeled,
  seeded, drained and chopped
juice of 1 lime or lemon
5 ml / 1 tsp salt
2.5 ml / 1/2 tsp freshly-ground pepper

Scoop out the avocado flesh into a bowl and mash until fairly smooth, retaining a little texture. Add the onion, garlic, coriander, chilli pepper, tomatoes and lime or lemon juice, salt and pepper. Mix well, add the reserved avocado stone, cover with cling film (plastic wrap) and chill until needed. Serve in a bowl, but don't forget to remove the stone before serving!

PATACONES

*T*hese plantain crisps, an authentic taste of Central and South America, are a real favourite with everyone, old and young. My brothers and I consumed hundreds of *patacones* when we lived in Colombia and they are so easy to make, especially if you have a deep-fryer. *Patacones* are a nutritious snack served with drinks, with dips, such as *Guacamole*, or as an accompaniment to a main course. Plantains are not green bananas, so be sure to buy the real thing. They are easy to find in Afro-Caribbean markets.

MAKES ABOUT 12 PATACONES
2 large plantains
sunflower oil for deep-frying
30 ml / 2 tbsp freshly-ground sea salt
1 clove garlic, crushed (optional)

Remove the skin from the plantains with a sharp knife and cut into 2.5 cm / 1 inch slices.
Heat the oil in a deep-fryer or wok to 180°C / 350°F or until it is hot enough to turn a cube of white bread golden in 1 minute. Slide half the plantain pieces into the oil, frying for about 2-3 minutes until golden. Remove with a slotted spoon and drain on absorbent kitchen paper (paper towels). Fry the remainder of the plantain in the same way and drain.
While the fried plantain is still warm, flatten to about 5 mm / ¼ inch thick. (I found that by putting the pieces one at a time between two saucers and pressing hard, the plantain gets squashed quite flat.) Sprinkle with a little salt and rub with garlic and deep-fry again in two batches for 1-2 minutes until golden-brown and crisp. Drain on absorbent kitchen paper (paper towels), sprinkle with plenty of salt and serve immediately.
If you want to prepare these in advance, do the preliminary frying, flatten and then finish just before serving.

DEEP-FRIED TOSTADAS WITH GUACAMOLE & RADISH

*T*hese very crispy fried tortillas can be served in many different ways and can either be round or triangular. The last time I made them, half my guests ate them all before the others arrived, so do make enough!

SERVES 6-8

For the Tostadas
140 g/5 oz (1¼ cups) wholemeal flour
7.5 ml/½ tsp salt
15 ml/1 tbsp mild chilli powder
2.5 ml/½ tsp ground cumin
2.5 ml/½ tsp ground coriander
freshly-ground black pepper
20 g/1½ tbsp vegetable shortening, cut into small cubes
150 ml/5 fl oz hot water
Vegetable oil to deep-fry

For the topping
20 radishes, finely grated
30 ml/2 tbsp white vinegar
salt and freshly-ground black pepper
1 recipe quantity *Guacamole* (page 150)
120 ml/4 fl oz Green Tomatillo Sauce (page 167) or a dash of Tabasco
1 handful coriander leaves

Mix the flour, salt and spices in a large bowl. Rub in the fat until the mixture resembles coarse breadcrumbs. Add the hot water slowly to form a pliable dough. Knead on a floured board until smooth, then cover with a warm, damp tea towel and leave for 5 minutes.

Divide the dough into 20 equal pieces and keep covered with a tea towel. Working with one piece at a time, shape into a ball and then flatten. Roll out very thinly, approximately 2 mm/⅛ inch. Using a pastry cutter or bowl, cut out a 12.5 cm/5 inch circle. Put the excess dough back in the bowl. Dust with flour and stack on a plate, covering with another damp towel. Continue in this way until you have used all the dough.

Heat a griddle or heavy frying pan. When a few drops of water sprinkled on the pan sizzle, start cooking the tortillas. Cook for about 40 seconds, until it begins to bubble, turn over and cook for a further 20 seconds.

Stack the cooked tortillas and cover with another tea towel.

When all the tortillas are cooked, heat a deep-fryer or wok half-filled with vegetable oil.

To make triangular *tostadas*, simply cut the cooked tortillas into quarters, then deep-fry in batches for about 1 minute, remove with a slotted spoon and drain on absorbent kitchen paper (paper towels). Alternatively, slip 2 whole circular tortillas into the hot oil, fry for 1 minute and drain.

To make the topping mix the radishes, vinegar, salt and pepper in a bowl. Prepare the *tostadas* by spreading with approximately 30 ml/2 tbsp guacamole, 15 ml/1 tbsp radish mixture and a little green tomatillo sauce or Tabasco. Garnish with coriander leaves.

MAKING TOSTADAS IN SAN CRISTOBAL CHIAPAS

CARROT, BEAN & RED PEPPER SALAD

*T*his tasty salad was served to me in a tiny restaurant nestled in the hills and mountains on the way to Chichicastenango, a small colonial village with a magnificent market on Thursday and Sunday. Many traders come from near and far to sell their freshest vegetables, fruit, flowers and spices as well as exotic masks used in local festivals and textiles of bright flowery and geometric designs in dazzling colours. The hustle and bustle in the town square on market days is formidable and I could not resist buying a bunch of carrots to sketch, after which I peeled and shared them, deliciously sweet and crunchy, with my travelling companions. For this salad, it is important to cut the vegetables into thin matchsticks and to cook until they are just tender.

SERVES 4-6

450 g/1 lb carrots, peeled
225 g/8 oz fine beans
2 red peppers
For the dressing:
30 ml/2 tbsp olive oil
30 ml/2 tbsp walnut oil
45 ml/3 tbsp white wine vinegar
1 clove garlic, finely chopped
juice of 1 lime or lemon
salt and freshly-ground black pepper

45 ml/3 tbsp walnuts, roughly chopped
30 ml/2 tbsp finely chopped fresh coriander
30 ml/2 tbsp finely chopped fresh parsley
15 ml/1 tbsp clear honey
2.5 ml/¹/₂ tsp mild or hot chilli powder

Cut the carrots into matchstick lengths. Top and tail the beans and cut into small pieces. Deseed the peppers, removing any white membrane and cut into thin matchstick lengths.

Put the carrots into a small quantity of boiling salted water and simmer until they are just tender, about 2-3 minutes. Refresh under cold running water and drain. Cook the beans similarly, refresh and drain.

Place the vegetables in a bowl. Mix all the dressing ingredients together, pour over the vegetables and mix well. Chill in the refrigerator for about 30 minutes before serving.

If you can find carrots that still have their foliage, you can use this to make an attractive border in a salad bowl and pile the salad in the centre.

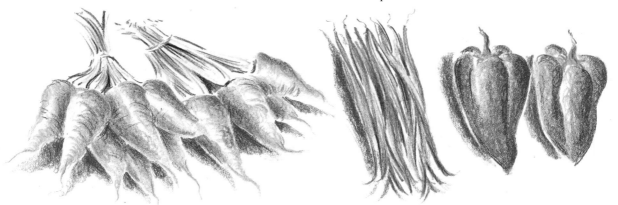

WOMEN OUTSIDE CHICHICASTENANGO

REFRIED BEANS

*B*eans are a staple food in Mexico. In the market of Merida, I watched many women peel the bean pods to reveal either black, red or pinto beans.
Refried beans are the consistency of mashed potatoes and they make a good accompaniment to any Mexican meal.

MAKES 600ML/1 PINT (20 FL OZ)

225 g/½ lb red kidney, black or pinto beans,
  soaked overnight
2 cloves garlic
10 ml/2 tsp sea salt
10 ml/2 tsp granulated sugar
45 ml/3 tbsp vegetable oil
2 small onions, chopped
2 fresh green jalapeño chilli peppers

Rinse the beans in 2-3 changes of cold water, place in a bowl, cover with enough water to come 12 cm/5 inches above the level of the beans and soak overnight.
Drain the beans. Fill a medium-sized deep saucepan with fresh water, add the beans, skewer the garlic on a cocktail stick and add to the beans. Simmer over a moderately high heat for up to 3 hours, until the beans feel very mushy and start to fall apart. You will need to top up the water frequently, but towards the end of the cooking time, allow the liquid to evaporate so that the consistency of the beans is like a paste. Remove and discard the garlic, add the salt and sugar and simmer gently for a further 10 minutes.
Meanwhile, heat 1 tbsp of the oil and fry one onion until golden. Add the onion and oil to the bean mixture. Add the chilli peppers, simmer for another 15 minutes, then remove and discard the chillies. If the mixture looks watery, simmer for a little longer.
Remove from the heat and leave to cool for at least 1 hour.
Then heat the remaining oil in a large, heavy frying pan and fry the rest of the onion until it is dark brown. Remove the onion and set aside. Add the beans, mashing them and stirring until they become a thick paste, adding a little more oil if they start to stick.
Remove from the heat and mix in the onion.
The mixture can be stored in the refrigerator for up to 5 days.

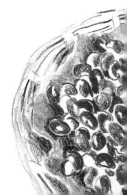

CAULIFLOWER WITH MOLÉ SAUCE

*M*ole is traditionally served with turkey in Mexico where *mulli* was the early name for sauce. This very rich sauce made with chocolate was created by a sister in the convent of St. Andrea de la Asuncion. I have adapted this traditional recipe to use as a sauce for cauliflower, but have omitted the dried chillies commonly used, but sometimes difficult to obtain outside Mexico. If you are lucky enough to have *ancho, mulato* and *pastilla* dried chillies to hand, use 4 of each, seeded, chopped and soaked in warm water for 30 minutes, then drained.

SERVES 4-6

2 cloves garlic
1 large cauliflower, cut into florets
For the sauce:
115 g / 4 oz / ¾ cup slivered almonds
60 g / 2 oz / ⅓ cup roasted peanuts
2.5 ml / ½ tsp coriander seeds
1.2 ml / ¼ tsp ground cloves
10 mm / ½ inch piece cinnamon stick
2.5 ml / ½ tsp aniseed
6 fresh green jalapeño chilli peppers
.5 litre / 16 fl oz warm water
2 medium-sized onions, chopped

2 garlic cloves, finely chopped
450 g / 1 lb ripe tomatoes, skinned, seeded and chopped or
    400 g / 14 oz tinned plum tomatoes, drained and chopped
85 g / 3 oz / ⅔ cup seedless raisins
120 ml / 4 fl oz vegetable oil
500 ml / 16 fl oz vegetable or chicken stock
60 g / 2 oz plain (semisweet) chocolate, broken

Bring a large saucepan of salted water to the boil. Add the garlic and cauliflower. Cook until the cauliflower is just tender. Drain, discard the garlic and set aside.
Make the sauce. In a food processor or blender, process the almonds, peanuts, coriander seeds, cloves, cinnamon, aniseed and half the sesame seeds. Turn into a bowl. Process to a thick paste the chillies, water, onions, garlic, tomatoes and raisins. Transfer to a bowl and mix with the processed nuts and spices.
Heat the oil in a saucepan over a moderate heat. Add the mixture and fry, stirring frequently until heated through. Add the stock and chocolate. Simmer until the chocolate has melted and the sauce is about the consistency of double cream. Cover and simmer gently for 20 minutes, stirring occasionally. Add the cooked cauliflower and simmer for 5 minutes.
Meanwhile, in a small frying pan, roast the remaining sesame seeds over a moderate heat until golden.
To serve, put the cauliflower and sauce into a warmed serving dish and sprinkle with the roasted sesame seeds. Serve immediately.

MEXICAN TOMATO SAUCE

*T*his sauce is used in Mexico with rice, fish or vegetables.

MAKES 480ML/16 FL OZ

15 ml / 1 tbsp olive oil

1 small onion, finely chopped

2 cloves garlic, finely chopped

450 g / 1 lb ripe tomatoes, skinned, seeded and
   chopped *or*

400 g / 14 oz tinned plum tomatoes, chopped

1 whole fresh green jalapeño chilli pepper

15 ml / 1 tbsp tomato paste

15 ml / 1 tbsp finely chopped fresh coriander

salt and freshly-ground black pepper

Heat the oil in a frying pan and fry the onion and garlic for 5 minutes, until transparent, but do not allow to brown. Add the tomatoes, tomato paste, coriander and chilli pepper. Season with salt and pepper and simmer, covered, for 20 minutes, or until thick. Remove the chilli pepper and serve.

GREEN RICE

A traditional dish, this rice goes very well with most Mexican food.

SERVES 4-6

1 small onion, roughly chopped

1 large green pepper, seeded and roughly
   chopped

2 cloves garlic, roughly chopped

30 ml / 2 tbsp finely chopped fresh parsley

45 ml / 3 tbsp finely chopped fresh coriander

45 ml / 3 tbsp olive oil

225 g / 8 oz (1¼ cups) long-grain rice

360 ml / 12 fl oz chicken or vegetable stock

salt and freshly-ground black pepper

6 fresh coriander leaves, chopped

Process the onion, green pepper, garlic, parsley and coriander in a food processor or blender until finely chopped. Heat 15 ml / 1 tbsp of the oil in a small saucepan. Add the onion-pepper mixture and cook, stirring, for about 3 minutes. Heat the remaining oil in a heavy frying pan. Add the rice and stir over a medium heat for about 3-4 minutes, until all the rice is coated in oil. Add the onion-pepper mixture, stock, salt and pepper and bring to the boil. Cover and simmer for 10 minutes. Reduce the heat and continue to cook, covered, for about 30 minutes, until the rice is tender and the stock has been absorbed. The rice should be cooked, but moist. Add more stock if necessary. Serve, garnished with chopped coriander.

AVOCADO SOUP

*T*his delicate and elegant pale green soup can be prepared in no time at all and served either warm or chilled on a hot summer day.

SERVES 6-8

4 ripe avocados
1.2 litres / 2 pints (40 fl oz) chicken or vegetable stock
15 ml / 1 tbsp lemon juice
salt and freshly-ground black pepper
45 ml / 3 tbsp finely chopped coriander

Cut 3 of the avocados in half lengthways, remove the stones (pits) and scoop the flesh into a blender or food processor. Heat the stock and pour into the blender, in batches if necessary and process with the avocado until very smooth. Peel and stone the remaining avocado and cut into thin slices for garnish.
Sprinkle with lemon juice. Return the soup to the pan and bring to just below boiling point. Add lemon juice, salt and pepper to taste and serve in individual bowls, sprinkled with coriander and a few slices of avocado. To serve cold, chill in the refrigerator for at least 1 hour.

YUCATAN PEPPERS STUFFED WITH CHICKEN

*T*his spicy main course dish is very good for entertaining as you can prepare the filling early in the day and fill and bake the peppers just 30 minutes before serving. Serve with *Green Rice* (page 158) or a salad.

SERVES 4

5 large green or red peppers
60 ml/4 tbsp olive oil
2 medium-sized onions, finely chopped
2 cloves garlic, crushed
2 small dried red chillies (chilli peppers), finely chopped
450 g/1 lb skinned boneless chicken breasts, chopped or minced
5 ml/1 tsp dried oregano
5 ml/1 tsp salt
2 bay leaves
2.5 ml/$^1/_2$ tsp Tabasco sauce
30 ml/4 tbsp flour
240 ml/8 fl oz chicken stock
45 ml/3 tbsp tomato paste
15 ml/1 tbsp finely chopped fresh coriander
5 ml/1 tsp ground cumin
2.5 ml/$^1/_2$ tsp ground cloves
30 ml/2 tbsp sugar
60 ml/2 fl oz dry sherry
85 g/3 oz/$^1/_2$ cup seedless raisins
coriander leaves (cilantro)

Cut 4 of the peppers in half lengthways, leaving the stalks on, carefully scoop out the pith and seeds and discard. Set the shells aside. Cut the remaining pepper in half, discard the seeds and white membrane and chop the flesh finely.

Heat the oil in a saucepan, add the onions, garlic, chillies and chopped pepper and fry until soft. Add the chicken, oregano. salt, bay leaves and Tabasco sauce and fry for about 5 minutes. Stir in the flour, then add the stock and tomato paste and bring to the boil. Add the coriander, cumin, cloves, sugar, sherry and raisins. Reduce the heat to low, cover and simmer for 30 minutes, stirring occasionally, until the mixture is quite thick. Remove from the heat and discard the bay leaves

Preheat the oven to 180°C/350°F/Mark 4. Carefully spoon the chicken mixture into the pepper halves and arrange in one layer in a shallow, well-greased baking dish. Bake for 30 minutes.

Garnish with coriander and serve immediately.

MARKET WOMAN IN MERIDA

STUFFED CHAYOTES

*C*hayotes, pear-shaped summer squash, appear occasionally on exotic market stalls or in supermarkets, but I did not know how to prepare them until I travelled through Chiapas, Mexico, where they are used in all manner of ways. Their skins range from pale to dark green and they have a pale green pulp, which has a very mild taste, not unlike pumpkin. Chayotes can be used for savoury as well as dessert dishes. This rather spicy recipe is perfect as a main course.

SERVES 4

4 chayotes

30 ml / 2 tbsp olive oil

2 cloves garlic, finely chopped

1 medium-sized onion, finely chopped

225 g / 8 oz chicken breast, cut into thin strips (optional)

1 dried red (serrano) chilli, seeded and finely chopped

3 ripe tomatoes, skinned and finely chopped

30 ml / 2 tbsp tomato paste

20 ml / 1 heaped tbsp cumin seeds

5 ml / 1 tsp mild or hot chilli powder

60 ml / 2 fl oz water

85 g / 3 oz / ¾ cup feta cheese, crumbled

60 ml / 4 tbsp breadcrumbs

60 ml / 4 tbsp cold water

75 ml / 5 tbsp soured cream to garnish

5 ml / 1 tsp dried oregano to garnish

Cook the chayotes in salted boiling water for 25-30 minutes or until tender (test by inserting a cocktail stick through the pointed end of the squash).

Heat the oil in a saucepan. Add the garlic, onion, chicken (if used) and chopped chilli and fry gently for 5 minutes, stirring frequently. Add the tomatoes, tomato paste, cumin, chilli powder and water. Cook uncovered over a gentle heat for 5 minutes, until thickened. Remove from the heat and set aside.

Cut a thin lengthways slice from one side each chayote, so that they sit level, then slice off the top third of each. Discard the seed and scoop out the flesh, leaving a .5 cm/¼ inch shell. Take care not to pierce the skin. Drain the chayote shells upside down on absorbent kitchen paper (paper towels). Drain and chop the flesh. Add to the chicken mixture with half the cheese and half the breadcrumbs and mix well. Spoon the filling into the shells, piling it high, then smooth the tops. Sprinkle with the remaining cheese and breadcrumbs.

Place the filled chayotes into a greased, shallow ovenproof dish. You can prepare the recipe up to this point in advance, cover with foil and set aside until 30 minutes before serving.

Preheat the oven to 190°C/375°F/Mark 5. Cook for 25 minutes, until golden-brown. Serve immediately, garnished with soured cream and oregano, accompanied by a salad.

FISH BAKED WITH CHILLI & TOMATOES

*T*his peasant dish from the eastern coast of Mexico makes a wonderful
main course for fish lovers served with green or plain rice.
Use the quantity of chilli you prefer, remembering that if you include the
seeds, the dish will be "hotter". The tomato sauce and marinade for the
fish can be prepared in advance, then it can all be assembled and baked
45 minutes before serving.

SERVES 6

For the tomato sauce:

90 ml / 3 fl oz olive oil

7 cloves garlic

2 large onions, finely chopped

1 kg / 2 lb ripe tomatoes, skinned and
finely chopped

150 ml / 5 fl oz fish stock

20 green olives, stoned and finely
chopped

30 ml / 2 tbsp drained capers

3 bay leaves

2.5 ml / $^1/_2$ tsp dried thyme

5 ml / 1 tsp dried oregano

2.5 ml / $^1/_2$ tsp dried marjoram

3 fresh green jalapeño chilli peppers,
seeded and chopped

salt and freshly-ground black pepper

To prepare the fish

juice of 1 lime

3 cloves garlic, crushed

2 bay leaves

2.5 ml / $^1/_2$ tsp dried oregano

45 ml / 3 tbsp olive oil

salt and freshly-ground black pepper

1 kg / 2 lb red snapper, John Dory or
other white-fleshed fish fillets,
skinned

fresh coriander and lime wedges to
garnish

Prepare the tomato sauce. Heat the oil in a saucepan and add 3 whole
cloves of garlic. When they are brown, remove and discard. Crush the
remaining 4 garlic cloves and add to the oil with the onion. Fry until the
onion is transparent. Add the tomatoes and the remainder of the sauce
ingredients and simmer for 45 minutes, covered, stirring occasionally. The
sauce should be thick. Remove from the heat and set aside.
While the sauce is cooking, prepare the fish. In a food processor, blend
the lime juice, garlic, bay leaves, oregano, oil, salt and pepper. Put the
fish into a deep dish, pour the marinade over and chill in the refrigerator
for at least 1 hour.
Preheat the oven to 200°C / 400°F / Mark 6. Pour some of the sauce into
the base of a baking dish, place the drained fish fillets on top and pour
the rest of the sauce over. Bake for 45 minutes until the fish is cooked.
Serve from the baking dish or on individual plates, with plenty of tomato
sauce, garnished with fresh coriander and lime wedges.

RED BEAN SOUP

*T*he colour of this soup is the most amazing rich red and the flavour is really earthy. I love it on a cold winter day; thick, and healthy, and, apart from the time needed to cook the beans, it is an easy soup to prepare.

SERVES 6-8

450 g / 1 lb dried red kidney beans, soaked overnight
5 ml / 1 tsp cumin seeds
15 ml / 1 tbsp coriander seeds
5 ml / 1 tsp dried oregano
1 medium-sized onion, peeled
4 large cloves garlic, lightly crushed
2 fresh green jalapeño chilli peppers, halved lengthways

1 small bunch fresh coriander
2 bay leaves
7.5 ml / 1½ tsp peppercorns
2.5 litres / 4 pints / 2½ quarts water
120 ml / 4 fl oz tomato paste
7.5 ml / 1½ tsp sea salt
45 ml / 3 tbsp goats' cheese, crumbled

Rinse the beans in 2-3 changes of cold water, place in a bowl, cover with enough water to come 12 cm / 5 inches above the level of the beans and soak overnight. Drain.

Roast the cumin and coriander seeds with the oregano either in a flat non-stick frying pan over a high heat, moving the pan as the spices roast, or in a hot oven (200°C / 400°F / Mark 6) for about 5 minutes, turning once. Remove from the heat and roughly grind the spices in a pestle and mortar or coffee grinder. Place the onions, garlic, chillies, coriander, bay leaves, thyme and peppercorns into a square of cheesecloth and tie up into a bouquet garni.

Bring the water to the boil in a medium-sized pan. Drain the beans and add to the pan with the tomato paste, bouquet garni and salt. Simmer over a very low heat for 2 - 2 ½ hours, or until the beans are very soft, adding water to the pan as necessary. Remove the bouquet garni and discard and leave the mixture to cool.

Put the beans and cooking liquid into a blender or food processor in batches and blend until very smooth. Return to the pan and heat, adding water as necessary to obtain the proper consistency.

Serve in individual bowls, garnished with crumbled goats' cheese and chopped coriander, accompanied by warm wheat tortillas or bread for a really filling lunch or supper.

This soup will keep in the refrigerator for up to 2 days.

FISH WITH GREEN TOMATILLO SAUCE

*T*omatillos, are an indispensable ingredient in Mexican cooking and are available tinned, but fresh ones are really worth looking for. They look a little like cape gooseberries with their papery husks and because of their colouring, are often thought of as unripe tomatoes.
This recipe makes a very elegant and tangy main course served with
Green Rice (page 158)

SERVES 4

1 litre / 2 pints (5 cups) water
12 medium tomatillos, husked
7 cloves garlic, peeled
4-6 fresh green jalapeño chilli
   peppers, stalks removed
¹/₂ onion, coarsely chopped
35 g / 1¹/₄ oz (³/₄ cup) fresh coriander

salt and freshly-ground black pepper
450 g / 1 lb fresh haddock or other
   white fish fillets
45 ml / 3 tbsp fresh lime juice
lemon wedges to garnish
sprigs of fresh coriander to garnish

Wash the tomatillos under cold running water. Bring the water to the boil and add the tomatillos, 4 garlic cloves, chilli peppers and onion. Cook, covered, over a moderate heat for 20 minutes. Drain, reserving the cooking liquid and allow to cool.
Meanwhile, process the remaining garlic with the coriander in a blender or food processor. Add the tomatillo mixture with a little of the cooking liquid and process again Add salt to taste. The sauce should be quite thick, so be careful not to add too much liquid.
Sprinkle the fish with lime juice, salt and pepper and leave to marinate for 5 minutes.
Preheat the oven to 200°C / 400°F / Mark 6. Heat the remaining oil in a large flat frying pan, Add the fish fillets and cook for just 1 minute on each side. Remove from the heat and place in a large, buttered oval ovenproof dish. Pour the hot tomatillo sauce over the fish and bake in the centre of the oven for 5-8 minutes, until just cooked. Serve garnished with lemon wedges and fresh coriander sprigs.

EMPANADAS WITH TOMATO & SHRIMP

*S*mall empanadas are perfect as appetizers, served hot with lemon wedges. Larger ones can provide the basis of a main meal, perhaps served with hot tomato sauce, salad and rice. I was raised on these delicious pasties, which are a little like samosas and are found all over Central and South America, filled with vegetables, spicy meat, chicken, fish or cheese.

In this recipe, the empanadas are baked, rather than fried; which gives one time to spend with guests.

MAKES ABOUT 18-20 SMALL EMPANADAS

For the filling:

100 ml / 3½ fl oz olive oil

3 cloves garlic, minced

1 medium-sized onion, finely chopped

2 fresh green jalapeño peppers, seeded and chopped

3 medium-sized ripe tomatoes, skinned, seeded and finely chopped

3.5 ml / ³⁄₄ tsp ground cumin

sea salt and freshly-ground black pepper

450 g / 1 lb small shrimp, shelled and deveined

For the dough:

200 g / 7 oz (1¾ cups) plain white flour

5 ml / 1 tsp salt

5 ml / 1 tsp black pepper

5 ml / 1 tsp mild or hot chilli powder

20 g / 4 oz (6 tbsp) butter, cut into small cubes

60 ml / 4 tbsp iced water

1 egg, lightly beaten

First make the filling. Heat the oil in a saucepan, add garlic and onion and fry until just brown. Add the chillis, tomatoes, cumin and salt and pepper to taste. Cook over a moderate heat for 40 minutes. Add the shrimp and cook for a further 10 minutes until the sauce is thick.

To make the dough. Sift the flour and salt into a large bowl and add the pepper and chilli powder. Rub in the butter until the mixture resembles coarse breadcrumbs. Slowly add the water and gather the dough into a compact ball. Cut into two pieces and roll out half the dough on a lightly floured surface, making a rough circle about 2 mm / ¹⁄₈ inch thick. Cut out small 75 cm / 3 inch circles with a biscuit cutter or the rim of a glass. Lightly dust with flour and stack the dough circles.

Preheat the oven to 200°C / 400°F / Mark 6.

Place about 5 ml / 1 tsp filling in the centre of each circle of dough. Brush the edges with a little water. Fold the empanada in half to enclose the filling and press the edges of the crescents firmly together. At this point they can be placed side by side on a dish covered with either cling film (plastic wrap) or aluminium foil and chilled in the refrigerator for several hours until ready to bake.

Place the empanadas on a greased baking sheet. Brush well with the beaten egg. Bake in the centre of the oven for 15 minutes, or until golden. Transfer to a heated serving dish and serve immediately, garnished with lemon wedges.

FRIED YUCCA

*Y*ucca, or cassava, is one of those root vegetables one sometimes sees at the market, wonders what it is and somehow never has the courage to try. However, it is delicious; a little like parsnip in flavour. Fried yucca is delicious served instead of roast potatoes, or as an appetizer with a dip.

SERVES 4
450 g / 1 lb yucca
30 ml / 2 tbsp sea salt
vegetable oil for deep-frying

Peel the yucca and cut each piece into quarters lengthways and into 7.5 cm / 3 inch lengths, to end up with large chips.
Cook in boiling water to cover until tender, about 15 minutes. Drain, cool and chill in the refrigerator for about 1 hour.
Heat the oil in a deep-fryer, wok or deep frying pan and fry the yucca in batches, until golden-brown. Drain on absorbent kitchen paper (paper towels) and repeat until you have fried all the yucca. Sprinkle with plenty of salt and pile onto a serving dish.
Alternatively, you can bake the yucca. Boil as above, then place in an ovenproof dish with 30 ml / 2 tbsp olive oil. Bake in the centre of a preheated oven (200°C / 400°F / Mark 6) until golden-brown, about 10-15 minutes. Serve sprinkled with plenty of salt.

CALIFORNIAN
Markets

The farmers' markets of California provided me with an enormous surprise. The climate of California so resembles the Mediterranean and here you will encounter a wealth of fresh produce with varieties of vegetables and herbs seldom seen together elsewhere in the world. In the market of Berkeley, on the outskirts of San Francisco, I saw huge mounds of bright yellow long courgettes (zucchini) as well as the small round Koboche variety, purple, yellow and green fine beans, baby sweetcorn, small bunches of beetroot and healthily-ripened red tomatoes. There were Persian, Thai and cinnamon basil in addition to the more common sweet basil. While I was busy contemplating the varieties of potatoes, my friends were busy showing me long, slim Japanese aubergines (eggplant) that were perfect for barbecuing plus fat, dark-mauve Italian examples and yellow and streaky-mauve small varieties.

These farmers' markets may not have the beautiful, romantic backdrops of Italy or France, but the keen farmers, who raise their crops organically, come dressed in bright T-shirts and baseball caps. They make their stalls as colourful as possible, displaying their produce with real pride and joy.

They are quite happy to chat about the latest method of growing red turnips, or to tell stories about how the original seeds for their sweet basil were brought over from Italy by their grandparents. One stallkeeper displayed hundreds of huge garlic strings; another was simply selling neat bunches of baby asparagus. One woman's stall was laden with bunches of Thai, cinnamon and sweet basil, plus a magnificent display of wild thyme, flat leaf parsley, coriander, tarragon and sage plants in terracotta pots. This all left me with the feeling that

FARMERS' MARKET IN SANTA BARBARA

these people really cared about what they were growing and selling.

After several days of enjoying the fabulous Napa Valley region, with its world-famous vineyards, vast olive groves and superb restaurants, I journeyed south by train to Santa Barbara. On the way, I passed vast fields of corn, strawberries, tomatoes and aubergines; beautiful, long, neat rows that disappeared into the distance, with farmers picking by hand in the same way as I had always seen in Europe. In Santa Barbara, I was taken by friends to the very lively weekly farmers' market, held in a large car parking lot, filled with marvellous produce. I sought out yellow fine beans, sun-dried tomatoes, yellow courgettes (which are just as tasty as green ones, but adding a visual surprise to salads), and a few big bunches of sweet basil. Once back in their home, I got chopping and made a simple supper consisting of Grated Courgette Salad, (page 174) and Tagliatelle with Sun-Dried Tomato Sauce, (page 180). Sitting on the terrace, overlooking the vast ocean below and the beautiful hills around, it could have been the Mediterranean.

California gives chefs a marvellous opportunity to create dishes using unusual and delicious sun-ripened ingredients, fusing flavours from East and West; healthy inspirations from the new world and the old. The Italian influence is especially strong here, because so many Italians emigrated, bringing with them their own cooking traditions. Today, the flavours of Thai, Mexican and Japanese cooking also seem to fuse together happily here to achieve an eclectic menu, which provides a style of cooking that is creative and tasty, always exploring new combinations.

CORN SOUP WITH BASIL

*C*orn grows profusely throughout California, and vast valleys are filled with these marvellously tall plants. I enjoyed the subtle and smooth taste of this soup which can be made in advance.

SERVES 4
4 corn on the cobs, cut in half crosswise
6 fresh bay leaves
freshly ground black pepper and salt
30 g / 1 oz butter
1 small onion, finely chopped
1 clove garlic, finely chopped
3 small tomatoes, skinned and chopped
900 ml / 1½ pts chicken or vegetable stock
150 ml / 5 fl oz double (heavy) cream
15 ml / 1 tbsp cumin seeds, freshly ground
12 fresh basil leaves, chopped

Bring a large pan of water to the boil and add the bay leaves and corn. Cook for about 20 minutes, or until the kernels are soft. Drain the corn cobs and leave to cool. Cut the corn off the cobs with a sharp knife. In a large saucepan melt the butter. Add the onion and garlic and cook gently for about 5 minutes until the onion is transparent.

Add the tomatoes. Simmer gently for 10 minutes. Add the stock and sweet corn kernels. Season to taste. Bring to the boil, then reduce the heat and simmer for 10 minutes. Pour the soup in a blender or food processor and process until smooth (you may need to do this in batches). Sieve the mixture into a saucepan. Stir in the cream and heat gently, making sure not to let the soup come to the boil. Add the cumin and stir well. Serve in individual bowls and garnish with the chopped basil. This soup is normally served hot, but it is also delicious cold on a hot summer day.

Spinach & Avocado Salad

A colourful and delicious salad, this can be served as a starter or as an accompaniment to pasta. Other salad leaves can be used, such as rocket or rughetta (arugala) or curly endive to create interesting variations.

SERVES 4

115 g/4 oz (2 cups) young, tender
  spinach
1 ripe avocado
15 ml/1 tbsp lemon juice
100 g/3½ oz roquefort cheese
½ head radicchio cut into wedges
30 g/1 oz (½ cup) fresh parsley,
  roughly chopped
30 g/1 oz (¼ cup) walnuts, roughly
  chopped

For the dressing:
30 ml/2 tbsp white wine vinegar
30 ml/2 tbsp sherry vinegar
30 ml/2 tbsp coarse-grained mustard
30 ml/2 tbsp walnut oil
30 ml/2 tbsp extra virgin olive oil
30 ml/2 tbsp sugar
salt and freshly ground black pepper

Wash the spinach thoroughly and drain well. Dry carefully.
Cut the avocado in half, remove the stone and skin, pour lemon juice over the flesh to prevent discolouration and cut into small slices. Cut the roquefort cheese into small dice. Place the spinach into a large salad bowl. Add the radicchio, parsley, walnuts, cheese and avocado. Make the dressing by mixing all the ingredients together in a bowl or shake in a jar with a tightly-fitting lid. Just before serving, pour the dressing over the salad and toss well.

Grated Courgette Salad

*T*his is a really quick and easy salad which I love to serve with grilled chicken or fish. Grated courgettes have a marvellous texture and the raspberry vinegar gives the salad "bite".

SERVES 4
900 g/2 lb courgettes
30 ml/2 tbsp raspberry vinegar
30 ml/2 tbsp extra virgin olive oil
15 ml/1 tbsp Dijon mustard
6 basil leaves, finely sliced
salt and freshly-ground black pepper
basil leaves to garnish

Grate the courgettes coarsely and put into a colander to drain for 10 minutes. Place in a serving dish.
Make the dressing by mixing the rest of the ingredients together in a bowl or shake in a jar with a tightly-fitting lid. Pour over the courgettes and mix well. Chill in the refrigerator and serve, garnished with basil leaves.

POTATO SALAD

A good potato salad is so popular for entertaining or for picnics. In this recipe, the new potatoes are cooked in their skins, marinated and then a light, fresh mayonnaise is folded in. Undercook the potatoes slightly so that they still have a "bite".

SERVES 4

670 g / 1½ lb new potatoes
120 ml / 4 fl oz sunflower oil
60 ml / 2 fl oz white wine vinegar
5 ml / 1 tsp Dijon mustard
5 ml / 1 tsp finely-chopped fresh basil leaves
1 large clove garlic, crushed
salt and freshly-ground black pepper
15 ml / 1 tbsp chopped fresh parsley

15 ml / 1 tbsp chopped fresh chives
For the mayonnaise:
1 egg yolk
1.25 ml / ¼ tsp Dijon mustard
sea salt and freshly-ground black pepper
90 ml / 3 fl oz sunflower oil
15 ml / 1 tbsp freshly-squeezed lemon juice

Wash the potatoes and cut them into pieces more or less the same size. Bring a saucepan of lightly-salted water to the boil, add the potatoes and cook until just tender when pierced with a knife, about 10 minutes. Remove from the heat, drain and put into a large bowl.

Prepare the marinade by mixing in a bowl or shaking in a jar with a tightly-fitting lid the oil, vinegar, mustard, basil, garlic, salt and pepper to taste. Pour the marinade over the potatoes while still warm and stir gently. Leave to cool for about 1 hour or refrigerate, covered, overnight.

To prepare the mayonnaise, whisk the egg yolk in a bowl until thick. Beat in the mustard, salt and pepper. Add the oil, drop by drop, whisking vigorously between each addition of oil, so that it is completely absorbed before adding the next drop. As the mayonnaise thickens and becomes shiny, the oil may be added in a thin stream. Finally, blend in the lemon juice and stir well.

Drain the marinade from the potatoes. Mix in the mayonnaise, parsley and chives. Chill in the refrigerator, covered with cling film (plastic wrap) for at least one hour.

SWORDFISH WITH TOMATILLO & RED PEPPER SAUCE

*T*wo classic sauces are used for this elegant dish which can either be a starter or main course. Serve the grilled (broiled) swordfish on a white plate with green tomatillo sauce on one side and red pepper sauce on the other.

SERVES 4

For the fish:

60 ml/4 tbsp extra virgin olive oil

2 cloves garlic, crushed

30 ml/2 tbsp fresh lime juice

30 ml/2 tbsp finely chopped fresh coriander

15 ml/1 tbsp freshly-ground black pepper

4 swordfish fillets (2 if using as a starter)

For the red pepper sauce:

2 large red peppers

30 ml/2 tbsp olive oil

3 cloves garlic, chopped

1 small onion, sliced

15 ml/1 tbsp balsamic vinegar

sea salt

30 g/1 oz (2 tbsp) butter

For the Green Tomatillo Sauce:

One-half the recipe quantity (page 167)

Make the marinade for the fish. Mix the oil, garlic, lime juice, coriander and pepper together. Place the fish fillets in a bowl, pour the marinade over, cover with cling film (plastic wrap) and marinate in the refrigerator for 2-3 hours.

Meanwhile, prepare the red pepper sauce. Place the peppers under a hot grill (broiler), turning them on all sides until the skin is all black and blistered. Remove from the grill, place in a bowl, covered with a tea towel and set aside for 30 minutes. When the peppers are cool enough to handle, remove and discard the skins, stems, cut in half and seed and remove any white membranes.

Put the oil, garlic, onion and peppers into a blender or food processor and process until smooth. Add the vinegar slowly. Turn the sauce into a saucepan and heat gently, adding the butter and salt to taste. Prepare the green tomatillo sauce.

Heat the grill (broiler). Remove the fish from the marinade and grill for approximately 4 minutes on the first side and 3 minutes on the other. To serve, place a swordfish fillet in the centre of the plate, pour the red pepper sauce on one side and the green sauce on the other. Both sauces can be prepared in advance and reheated just before serving.

SPINACH & CHEESE FILO PARCELS

*T*hese parcels are a treat to make and friends always comment on how tasty they are. They can be prepared in advance, in which case give them an initial 10 minutes in the oven, allow to cool and then reheat in a hot oven for 5 minutes, or until golden.

MAKES APPROXIMATELY 24 PARCELS

450 g / 1 lb fresh spinach
85 g / 3 oz (½ cup) ricotta cheese
100 g / 3½ oz (½ cup) feta cheese, crumbled
  or finely chopped
30 ml / 2 tbsp finely-chopped fresh mint
15 ml / 1 tbsp finely-chopped fresh parsley
30 ml / 2 tbsp pine nuts
zest of 1 lemon, finely grated 1.25 ml / ¼ tsp
  freshly-grated nutmeg
salt and freshly-ground black pepper
10 filo pastry sheets 25 cm / 10 inches square
55 g / 2 oz (½ stick) butter, melted
6-8 sprigs fresh mint leaves to garnish

Wash the spinach thoroughly and drain. Put into a large saucepan with only the water clinging to its leaves. Cook over a low heat until the spinach wilts, about 5 minutes. Drain well and leave to cool, then squeeze out as much liquid as possible.

Finely chop the spinach. Place the spinach in a large bowl with the ricotta and feta cheese, mint, parsley, pine nuts, lemon zest, nutmeg, salt and pepper and mix thoroughly.

Line an oven tray with nonstick greaseproof (waxed) paper. Preheat the oven to 200°C / 400°F / Mark 6.

Take one sheet of filo pastry and brush with melted butter. Lay another sheet directly on top and cut into 4 squares. Place 15 ml / 1 tbsp spinach filling in the centre of each square, brush the edges lightly with a little more butter and close by bringing the sides up, gathering in the centre and twisting the parcels. Continue to make all the filo parcels in the same way and place on the prepared oven tray. Brush all over with melted butter and bake in the oven for 15-20 minutes, until golden and crisp.

Serve as a starter by placing 3-4 parcels on an individual plate over a pool of Tomato Sauce, (page 26) and decorate with whole mint leaves.

TOMATO, CUCUMBER & FETA CHEESE SALAD

*T*his classic salad is splendid for picnics or a buffet.

SERVES 4-6

450 g / 1 lb cucumbers

3 small tomatoes, quartered

4 spring onions (scallions), finely sliced

250 g / 8 oz feta cheese, cut into small dice

30 ml / 2 tbsp finely-chopped fresh mint leaves

15 ml / 1 tbsp finely-chopped fresh chives

15 ml / 1 tbsp finely-chopped fresh thyme

30 ml / 2 tbsp white wine vinegar

30 ml / 2 tbsp extra virgin olive oil

salt and freshly ground black pepper

Cut the cucumber in quarters lengthways and then into 1.25 cm / ¼ inch slices and place in a large salad bowl. Add the tomatoes, spring onions, feta cheese and herbs and mix well.
Whisk together the vinegar, olive oil and seasoning, pour the dressing over the salad and mix well.
Serve chilled.

GAZPACHO

*T*his cold soup, originally from Spain, is also equally at home on the West Coast, where its flavour and simplicity is much appreciated.

SERVES 6

900 g / 2 lb large, ripe tomatoes

½ cucumber, peeled and chopped

½ red pepper, deseeded and chopped

½ green pepper, deseeded and chopped

2 cloves garlic, chopped

450 ml / 15 fl oz tomato juice

90 ml / 3 fl oz extra virgin olive oil

90 ml / 3 fl oz red wine vinegar

sea salt and freshly-ground black pepper

For the garnish:

½ red pepper, de-seeded finely chopped

½ green pepper, de-seeded finely chopped

½ cucumber, peeled and chopped

small croutons, fried in olive oil

Put the tomatoes in a bowl and cover with boiling water. Leave for 2-3 minutes, then slip off the skins and cut into halves. Put the tomatoes, cucumber, peppers, garlic and tomato juice into a blender or food processor (in batches as necessary) and process at high speed, until the mixture is smooth, adding the olive oil and vinegar while blending. Add salt and pepper to taste and chill in the refrigerator for at least 1-2 hours. For the garnish, serve pepper, cucumber and croutons in individual bowls.

TAGLIATELLE WITH SUN-DRIED TOMATO SAUCE

*S*un-dried tomatoes are such a delicious ingredient and Californians love using them. This is a hearty sauce which can be used with fresh or dried pasta and a variety of other dishes.

SERVES 4-6

450 g / 1 lb tagliatelle
45 ml / 3 tbsp olive oil
3 large cloves garlic, crushed
1 large onion, finely sliced
4 anchovy fillets, chopped
100 g / 3½ oz sun-dried tomatoes in oil,
  roughly chopped
400 g / 14 oz tinned plum tomatoes,
  chopped (juice reserved)
30 ml / 2 tbsp green peppercorns
7.5 ml / 1½ tsp chilli powder
5 ml / 1 tsp dried thyme
salt and freshly-ground black pepper

Heat the oil in a medium-sized saucepan over a moderate heat and gently fry the garlic, onion and anchovies until the onion is transparent.
Add the sun-dried tomatoes, tinned tomatoes with juice, green peppercorns, chilli powder, thyme and salt and pepper to taste. Cook for 10 minutes.
Meanwhile, place the tagliatelle in a large pan of lightly-salted boiling water. Cook dried pasta according to packet directions and fresh tagliatelle for 3-4 minutes until it is *"al dente"* (to the bite). Drain and put the tagliatelle into the sauce pan and mix well.
Serve immediately.

SUN-DRIED TOMATO TARTLETS

*T*his is an stunning warm appetizer to serve with drinks or as a starter with Spinach & Avocado Salad, (page 174). Filo pastry is readily available from most supermarkets and delicatessens. You can vary the size of the tartlets, depending on what size moulds you have available.

SERVES 4 (MAKES 16 TARTLETS)

16 sun-dried tomatoes in oil
8 anchovy fillets
1 egg yolk
120 ml / 4 fl oz double (heavy) cream
120 ml / 4 fl oz milk
sea salt and freshly-ground black pepper
8 filo pastry sheets cut into 20 cm / 8 inch
   squares
melted butter

Preheat the oven to 180°C / 350°F / Mark 4.
Roughly chop the tomatoes and cut the anchovy fillets into quarters. In a bowl, whisk together the egg yolk, cream, milk, salt and pepper. Cut each pastry square into quarters. Place a filo pastry square into each tartlet mould. Then place another one diagonally over it to make an 8-sided star. Put a small spoonful of tomato, 2 anchovy pieces and a portion of basil in each tartlet. Gently pour the egg mixture into each mould just up to the rim. Brush a little melted butter along the edge of the pastry.
Bake in the oven for 15 minutes, until the pastry is just golden.
Serve warm.

GRILLED AUBERGINES WITH PESTO & GOATS' CHEESE

*T*his dish makes an elegant starter, reminiscent of the flavours of the Mediterranean. Serve about 3 slices on individual plates with a couple of basil leaves as garnish.

SERVES 4
2 large aubergines (eggplant)
75 ml / 5 tbsp olive oil
3 cloves garlic, peeled and thinly sliced
150 g / 5 oz goats' cheese, thinly sliced
15 ml / 1 tbsp dried oregano
100 g / 3½ oz (½ cup) *pesto* (page 28)
8 basil leaves to garnish

Wash the aubergines and remove the stems. Slice thickly across, sprinkle generously with salt, put in a colander or sieve and leave for 30 minutes to drain. Rinse well and pat dry with absorbent kitchen paper (paper towels).

Heat half the oil in a large frying pan and add the garlic. Fry the aubergine slices in batches until golden-brown on both sides. Remove from the pan with a slotted spoon and drain on absorbent kitchen paper, adding more oil to the pan as needed until all the aubergine slices are fried. (This can be done in advance up to this stage if desired.)

Just before serving, heat the grill (broiler) to high. Place the fried aubergine slices on a foil-covered baking tray (cookie sheet) and spread a good helping of pesto on each slice. Then place a thin slice of goats' cheese on each. Sprinkle with the oregano and place under the grill for 4-5 minutes or until the cheese is melted and golden. Remove from the oven, place on individual plates, garnish with basil and serve immediately.

SPINACH & RICOTTA ROULADE

*T*his is a delightful light starter, which can be prepared in advance. I like to serve slices of this roulade either warm on a pool of Tomato Sauce, (page 26) or cold, on its own for a picnic or buffet.

SERVES 6

For the roulade:
450 g / 1 lb fresh spinach
45 g / 1½ oz butter
1 small onion, finely chopped
45 ml / 3 tbsp plain white flour
360 ml / 12 fl oz milk
30 ml / 2 tbsp freshly-grated parmesan
  cheese
4 large eggs, separated
salt and freshly-ground black pepper

2 large pinches nutmeg
For the filling:
225 g / 8 oz ricotta cheese
30 ml / 2 tbsp soured cream
½ red pepper, finely chopped
2 pinches cayenne pepper
salt and freshly-ground black pepper
15 ml / 1 tbsp finely-chopped fresh
  parsley

Lightly grease a 22.5 -35 cm / 9 14inch roulade (Swiss roll) tin and line with lightly greased paper.

Wash the spinach thoroughly and drain. Put into a large saucepan with only the water clinging to its leaves. Cook over a low heat until the spinach wilts, about 5 minutes. Drain well and leave to cool, then squeeze out as much liquid as possible.

In a saucepan, melt the butter and gently fry the onions until transparent, about 5 minutes. Stir in the flour and cook for 1 minute, then gradually blend in the milk. Bring to the boil, reduce the heat and cook for 2 minutes, stirring constantly. The sauce should be quite thick. Remove from the heat.

Preheat the oven to 200°C / 400°F / Mark 4. Chop the spinach and stir into the sauce. Add the cheese. Whisk the egg yolks and add to the mixture with the salt, pepper and nutmeg and mix well. Whisk the egg whites until stiff, but not dry and lightly fold into the mixture. Spread onto the prepared tin, level the surface and bake in the oven for 25 minutes, or until set and firm to the touch.

Meanwhile, in a bowl, mix together the ingredients for the filling. Once the roulade is baked, remove from the oven and leave to cool. Turn the roulade upside-down onto a sheet of lightly greased greaseproof (waxed) paper. Loosen the lining paper and remove carefully. Spread the filling as evenly as possible, using a palette knife. Roll up tightly, starting from the short side.

Serve hot on a pool of tomato sauce or cold.

YELLOW & GREEN COURGETTE SALAD

*Y*ellow courgettes (zucchini) are an exciting change from the usual green ones and this salad is ideal for a light summer lunch.

SERVES 4-6

450 g / 1 lb yellow courgettes, thinly sliced
450 g / 1 lb green courgettes, thinly sliced
30 ml / 2 tbsp extra virgin olive oil
30 ml / 2 tbsp white wine vinegar
15 ml / 1 tbsp walnut oil
15 ml / 1 tsp Dijon mustard
salt and freshly-ground black pepper
15 ml / 1 tbsp capers, roughly chopped
12 basil leaves, thinly sliced

Place the courgettes in a large salad bowl. Prepare the dressing by mixing the remaining ingredients except the garnish in a bowl or by shaking in a jar with a tightly-fitting lid. Pour over the courgettes and mix well.
Chill the salad and serve garnished with several basil leaves.

LASAGNE WITH FENNEL & SMOKED SALMON

*T*his rather light lasagne is a good choice for an elegant dinner party. I often prepare it the night before and reheat it just before serving. Fresh pasta really makes a difference in this recipe, which I serve with a parmesan sauce, sprinkled with fennel seeds and garnished with a few fresh fennel fronds.

For the pasta:

280 g / 10 oz (2½ cups) plain white flour

generous pinch of salt

3 large eggs, lightly beaten

15 ml / 1 tbsp olive oil

or 12 sheets of commercial fresh or dried lasagne noodles

For the filling:

1.1 kg / 2½ lb fennel bulbs

1 recipe quantity bechamel sauce (page 38)

240 ml / 8 fl oz fish stock

30 ml / 2 tbsp Pernod (optional)

250 g / 8 oz smoked salmon or salmon trimmings, thinly sliced

30 ml / 2 tbsp fennel seeds

60 ml / 4 tbsp freshly-grated parmesan cheese

sea salt and freshly-ground black pepper

For the sauce:

150 ml / 5 fl oz double (heavy) cream

45 ml / 3 tbsp freshly-grated parmesan cheese

15 ml / 1 tbsp fennel seeds

Make the pasta dough by mixing the flour, eggs, salt and olive oil together in a bowl until you get a coarse paste. Gather up into a ball, turn onto a lightly floured surface and knead until smooth and elastic, about 10 minutes. Cover with cling film (plastic wrap) and allow to rest for 30 minutes.

Meanwhile, cut the feathery fronds off the fennel, reserving them for garnish. Cut the bulbs in half crossways and cook in lightly salted boiling water for 15 minutes, until tender. Refresh under cold running water and drain. Cut into thin lengthways slices and set aside.

Take the pasta dough and divide into 4 equal pieces. Roll each into a ball and, one at a time, roll out on a lightly floured surface until it is approximately 2 mm / ⅛ inch thick. Cut into rectangles approximately 7.5 x 15 cm / 3 x 6 inches. Continue until all the pasta is rolled out and cut. Bring a large pan of salted water to the boil and add a spoonful of olive oil. Cook the lasagne, 2 sheets at a time, for 2 minutes, remove from the pan with a slotted spoon, plunge into a bowl of cold water and drain on separate sheets of absorbent kitchen paper (paper towels).

Preheat the oven to 180°C / 350°F / Mark 4. Make the bechamel sauce, adding the fish stock and Pernod, if using, at the last minute.

To assemble, grease a rectangular ovenproof dish with butter and place strips of pasta into the base, slightly overlapping. Build up with layers of fennel, salmon, bechamel sauce, fennel seeds and parmesan cheese, ending with a layer of pasta, bechamel, fennel seeds and parmesan cheese. Bake for 25-30 minutes until golden on top.

To make the parmesan sauce, heat the cream and parmesan cheese in a small saucepan until the cheese is melted, about 2-3 minutes. Season with salt and pepper.

To serve, cut a square of lasagne, place on an individual warmed plate, pour a little parmesan sauce on one side and sprinkle with a few fennel seeds. Garnish with the reserved fennel fronds.

HALIBUT WITH FENNEL & ONIONS

*T*he delicate texture of halibut is marvellously set off by this intensely flavoured sauce.

SERVES 4

For the marinade:
60 ml / 4 tbsp olive oil
2 cloves garlic, crushed
juice of ¹/₂ lemon
15 ml / 1 tbsp ground fennel seeds
sea salt and freshly-ground black pepper
4 halibut steaks, approximately 225 g / 8 oz each

For the sauce:
75 ml / 5 tbsp olive oil

2 medium-sized red onions, finely sliced
4 anchovy fillets, chopped
2 fennel bulbs thinly sliced
360 ml / 12 fl oz dry white wine
30 ml / 2 tbsp fennel seeds
juice of 1 lemon
sea salt and freshly-ground black pepper
chopped fennel fronds to garnish

First prepare the marinade. Combine all the ingredients, place the fish steaks in a dish and pour the marinade over. Cover with cling film (plastic wrap) and refrigerate for at least 1 hour.

To prepare the sauce, heat the oil in a medium-sized saucepan and fry the onions over a moderate heat until transparent. Add the anchovies and cook for 1 minute, then add the fennel and cook for 5 minutes. Pour in the wine, increase the heat to moderately high and cook, uncovered until the wine has reduced by one-half and the fennel is tender, approximately 20 minutes. Add the fennel seeds and lemon juice and cook, stirring, for a further 10 minutes. The sauce should now be quite thick.

Heat the grill (broiler) to high. Drain the excess marinade from the fish and lay it on a foil-covered baking tray (cookie sheet). Grill for 5-6 minutes, then turn over and grill for a further 3-4 minutes, until cooked. To serve, place a fish steak on a warmed plate, pour a little sauce on one side and garnish with fennel fronds.

CARROT & NUT CAKE

*T*his light and moist carrot cake is a favourite with my family. For a special treat, serve it with fresh whipped cream, laced with a dash of Armagnac or brandy.

7 large eggs, separated
225 g/8 oz caster sugar
170 g/6 oz (1½ cups) hazelnuts
 (filberts), finely ground
225 g/8 oz carrots, peeled and finely
 grated

5 ml/1 tsp baking powder
2.5 ml/½ tsp vanilla essence
2.5 ml/½ tsp almond essence
2.5 ml/½ tsp ground cinnamon
115 g/4 oz/1 cup fine breadcrumbs
15 ml/1 tbsp sugar

Preheat the oven to 180°C/350°F/Mark 4.
Line a 20 cm/8 inch baking tin with greaseproof paper and grease well.
Mix the egg yolks with the sugar in a bowl until creamy. Add the hazelnuts, carrots, baking powder, vanilla and almond essence and cinnamon and mix well.
In a separate bowl, whisk the egg whites and 15 ml/1 tbsp sugar until stiff, but not dry, then carefully fold in the carrot mixture. Pour into the prepared tin and bake for 50-55 minutes. Turn out of the tin and leave to cool on a wire rack before serving.

ACKNOWLEDGEMENTS

I would like to thank firstly all the market people who allowed me to draw them, and who answered numerous questions about the local produce and their region. Without them, this book would never have been possible.

A very special thanks to Maureen Green, my publisher, who has always had enormous faith in me and whose support has been tremendous throughout this whole project. Also to Stephen Singer who spent many hours testing recipes in my kitchen, and sustaining me with enthusiasm and cups of tea. Numerous friends tested a succession of sometimes unlikely sounding dishes, and special thanks to Evelyn, Alan, Sara, Max and Stefan Beazley, Eliana and Ray Thompkins, Jill Sudbury, Kim Dambaek, Louis Rivas Sanchez, Antonio Moreno, John and Emilia Scanlan, Alby Merry, Pep Reiff, Lyndon Alley and Roslin Wright. My thanks to Isobel Brown for sharing such wonderful times in the markets and over the dinner tables of Normandy, and to Janet Coles, Martin Smith, Dominique and Patrick Morsoom, Maureen and Tim Green for sharing their lovely homes in France with me and for their inspiration.

To my friend Yvonne Wensley for trekking around numerous Mexican and Guatemalan markets with me and helping to keep my pencils sharp! Antonio Salamida, Alberto Marra, Vittorio and Silvia for their wonderful hospitality and delicious cooking in Italy. To Janet and Nigel Konstam, Maddalena Bonino, Lina and Daniel for sharing their family recipes and to Diane Seed for her initiation to many new regions of Italy.

In Morocco, my thanks to all at the Villa Maroc, Essouira, most especially Amina, for her wondrous cooking and to all at the Palais Salam in Taroudant. In India, Chef Satish Arora at the Taj Mahal Hotel, Bombay, Chef Arun Chopra at the Taj Mahal Hotel, Delhi and Mr Peter Nathaniel of Claridges Hotel, Delhi were most helpful and enthusiastic in sharing their recipes. I would also like to thank Pushpa Prashar, Shaheen Rashid and Mel Watson who shared favourite Indian family recipes and endless hospitality.

In Thailand, my thanks to all at the Tara Tong Restaurant, the Royal Orchid Sheraton Hotel, Bangkok, to Sarayuth Atibodhi at the Oriental Hotel, Bangkok and to Vatcharin Bhumichitr, Sally and Gerry Marden who prepared marvellous food. Annibale Grassi for being a great guide.

Special thanks to George Young, Phil Wood, Jo Ann Deck and Fuzzy of Ten Speed Press for inspiring me in California and to Rick Weedn for exploring with me many West Coast markets. My thanks to Judy Dooling, my agent, who encouraged me endlessly and listened attentively and to Pamela Burden for all her typing and great encouragement. Finally, to my mother, who has been such an inspiration and has taught me the art of cooking and the appreciation of good food.

INDEX